D1014731

IMPLEMENTING A HUMAN DEVELOPMENT STRATEGY

Implementing a Human Development Strategy

Keith Griffin
*Professor of Economics and Chairman of
the Department of Economics
University of California, Riverside*

and

Terry McKinley
*Assistant Professor
International Development Program
of the School of International Service
American University, Washington, D.C.*

Foreword by
Mahbub ul Haq
Special Adviser to UNDP Administrator

St. Martin's Press   New York

First published in the United States of America in 1994

Printed in Great Britain

ISBN 0–312–12179–2

Library of Congress Cataloging-in-Publication Data
Griffin, Keith B.
Implementing a human development strategy / Keith Griffin and
Terry McKinley.
p.   cm.
Includes bibliographical references and index.
ISBN 0–312–12179–2
1. Economic development.   2. Community development.   3. Human
capital.   4. Quality of life.   5. Sustainable development.
I. McKinley, Terry.   II. Title.
HD82.G677   1994
338. 9—dc20   94–5976
                                                          CIP

This work was initially produced for UNDP as a part of
UNDP's Country Human Development Initiatives.

Contents

v

Foreword

Far from being a dismal science, Economics was always concerned with people and their welfare. The writings of Adam Smith, Karl Marx and John Maynard Keynes bear ample testimony to this statement. But something tragic happened to development economics on its way: it became dehumanised. In the new obsession with measuring national income accounts, human lives were often forgotten. In a way, the new emphasis on human development during the last few years arose as a protest against this unnecessary and unforgivable neglect.

The concept of human development makes it quite clear that the primary objective of development is to benefit people – to improve the quality of life available to all. Expansion of income and employment are essential. But they are only the means, not the end, of development. The end of development is to enlarge human capabilities and to widen the range of human choices. Income is only one of those choices, and a necessary one: it is far from being the sum total of human life. Other human choices include long, healthy, creative lives in a rich natural environment and a democratic civil society.

For some time now, development has been treated as synonymous with the growth in gross national product (GNP). While it is true that access to income may permit exercise of many other human options, the wellbeing of a society depends on the uses of this income rather than on its level. There are several country cases of high levels of human development at modest income levels and poor levels of human development at fairly high income levels. Moreover, the growing human distress and environmental deterioration even in rich nations is a constant reminder that high income levels, by themselves, are no guarantee of human progress.

There is no automatic link between economic growth and human progress. The concept of human development brings economic growth and human lives together. It is concerned with the processes through which human capabilities are built, how people participate in economic growth, and how they benefit from an increase in national production. Linking economic conditions and human lives is the central concern of human development.

The concept of human development weaves development models around people rather than people around development models. It raises some profound questions about the very character and distribution of economic growth.

Human development has two sides. It focuses equally on the formation of human capabilities (through investing in people) and on the use of those capabilities (through creating a participatory framework for income and employment growth). Unless the scales of human development finely balance the two sides, much human frustration can result.

Some have seen human development as 'human resources development'. But investing in people, or in human capital formation, is only one aspect of human development. It leaves out all discussion of human participation in growth, through employment and income generation, as well as wider aspects of a civil society.

Others have presented human development as a sectoral issue – as investment in health, education and other social services. But human development is a multisectoral, macroeconomic policy concern. Its ultimate objective is to ensure that economic growth translates into the improved wellbeing of people.

There are some who believe that there is a fundamental conflict between the concepts of economic growth and human development. Nothing can be further from the truth. Economic growth is a necessary, but not a sufficient, condition for human development. The quality of this economic growth is as important as its quantity. The concept of human development is concerned with both aspects of growth, with much more emphasis on the qualitative aspects. The basic theme of this new concept is that development must be much more than just the expansion of income and wealth. Its focus must be on people. And its principal objectives must be a significant reduction in poverty and a more equitable access to economic opportunities.

There is another dimension of development which is just as important. Development must be sustainable. It must protect the options of unborn generations. It must not run down the natural resource base needed for sustaining development in the future, or destroy the richness of nature which adds so much to life.

So human development must be sustainable development as well. For models of sustainable human development, it is necessary to maintain and regenerate all forms of capital – physical, human and natural. Running down any part of this capital heritage, without replenishing it, is like stealing from our own children.

Many of these ideas and concepts emerged in the *Human Development Reports*, issued by the UNDP since 1990, which I have had the great privilege of coordinating and launching. We were extremely fortunate in attracting an outstanding group of development professionals to contribute to these Reports, including Drag Avramovic, Meghnad Desai, Just Faaland, Azizur Rahman Khan, Graham Pyatt, Gustav Ranis, Amartya Sen, Frances Stewart, Paul Streeten and Wouter Tims. One of the moving spirits in this group has been Keith Griffin, who was involved, right from the beginning, in the evolution of the concept of human development and the formulation of practical country strategies for the implementation of this concept.

We invited Keith Griffin (in collaboration with Terry McKinley) in the summer of 1992 to review the evolution of ideas in the first three *Human Development Reports* (1990–92), as well as in the country human development strategies for Bangladesh, Colombia, Ghana and Pakistan which had been prepared with UNDP technical assistance. The main idea was to prepare a readable summary of the development dialogue which was beginning to take shape on the issues of human development and to present to the policymakers the key ideas in this field. We were highly pleased that Keith Griffin and Terry McKinley undertook this task and produced a monograph in October 1992 which first appeared as an Occasional Paper of the Human Development Report Office of UNDP.

I believe that Keith Griffin and Terry McKinley have done an outstanding job in distilling the real essence of the human development debate so far. Readers will find in these pages a very lucid, creative and highly readable version of many of the ideas that have taken shape through the medium of the *Human Development Reports* during the last four years. Busy policymakers all over the world will find this an indispensable primer.

The chief virtue of this volume is that it seeks to place human concerns at the very centre of the development debate and to move the study of economics once again closer to its primary objective.

New York

Mahbub ul Haq
Special Adviser to UNDP Administrator

Preface

The first version of this monograph was prepared for the United Nations Development Programme (UNDP) as a contribution to the work of the Human Development Report Office (HDRO). It was circulated by HDRO as its Occasional Paper No. 6 under the title *Towards a Human Development Strategy*. We are very grateful to Inge Kaul, the Director of HDRO, for her encouragement and assistance and for permission to publish the present version.

The original idea for this study came from Mahbub ul Haq, the Special Adviser to the Administrator of UNDP. A number of country studies had been commissioned by UNDP that contained specific recommendations for implementing a human development strategy. Dr Haq asked us to write a synthesis of those studies, a handbook that might be useful to policymakers in other countries interested in human development. In the event, a synthesis proved to be impossible, and what eventually emerged is what is before you. Dr Haq was sufficiently pleased by the result that he agreed to write a Foreword and we are very grateful to him for this gesture of solidarity.

A large number of people have read drafts of this study – United Nations Resident Representatives, leaders and members of missions that prepared country studies, headquarters staff of UNDP, our students and colleagues – and we are grateful to all of them for their comments, criticisms and suggestions. It goes without saying, but we must say it in any case, that the views expressed are our own and should not be interpreted as representing those of UNDP.

Introduction

The purposes of this short monograph are, first, to introduce the general reader to the basic concepts of human development, seen as an all-embracing strategy of development, and, second, to devise guidelines for use by national policymakers, development specialists and international advisers in constructing development strategies which give high priority to human development. Our intention is not to present a blueprint for human development that can be applied mechanically in every country but to raise the issues that must be addressed and to offer suggestions as to how these issues can be resolved. The point of departure for each country is, necessarily, distinct and reflects its history, culture, resource endowment and political institutions. Thus each country faces a unique set of problems, but also a unique set of opportunities and a unique set of feasible policies. There is more than one path to human development, and hence the need to consider alternative strategies, but any successful strategy will have to pay careful attention to the structure of incentives that guides economic activity, the allocation of public expenditure and the institutional arrangements that determine the distribution of wealth and income and the vulnerability of various sections of the population to events which can threaten their livelihood and perhaps even their life.

We begin, in Chapter 1, with an analysis of the essential features of a human development strategy. We regard human development as the end or objective of development. It is a way to fulfill the potential of people by enlarging their capabilities, and this necessarily implies empowerment of people, enabling them to participate actively in their own development. Human development is also a means since it enhances the skills, knowledge, productivity and inventiveness of people through a process of human capital formation broadly conceived. Human development is thus a people-centred strategy, not a goods-centred or production-centred strategy of development.

A people-centred strategy of development has implications for the role of the state. Often the discussion is couched in terms of the degree of centralisation of the public administration, with most analysts favouring a highly decentralised system of governance. We argue, however, that the appropriate degree of administrative decentralisation is a secondary issue. What really matters is the empowerment of local people to identify their own priorities and to implement programmes and projects of direct benefit to them. That is, development should be seen as a process that is not just for people but a process organised, guided and undertaken by people. This in turn implies the active participation of people in the development process and the consequent need to construct institutions that permit and indeed encourage that participation. A vigorous civil society, in other words, is an essential component of a successful human development strategy.

The strengthening of civil society need not imply a smaller role for government. Indeed we argue that the volume of public expenditure is less important than its composition. Human development is partly about changing spending priorities, not between the private and public sectors, but within the public sector itself. What matters, in other words, is what government does, not how big it is. In most developing countries much can be done to promote human development by reallocating government expenditure without the need to raise additional revenue through taxation. Of course, if government does more in some areas without raising taxes, it will have to do less in other areas. This in turn means that the distribution of the benefits and burdens of public-sector activities will alter – some groups will gain and others will lose – and hence it will be necessary to build political support for human development by creating effective coalitions of potential beneficiaries. Human development is not politically neutral; it is not a technocratic solution to development problems; it requires broadly-based popular support.

Some policies, however, are likely to be politically more controversial than others and consequently more difficult to implement. In Chapter 2 we discuss the set of incentives faced by producers and consumers. In principle, policies affecting incentives – essentially changes in relative prices and barriers to access – may often be less difficult to implement since they require neither a higher overall tax burden, nor a major reallocation of public expenditure, nor the creation of new institutions, nor the mounting of new programmes. Even so, changes in the set of incentives can be expected to encounter resistance because any change in relative prices or in access will alter not only the allocation of resources but also the distribution of income, and in some instances the changes in the distribution of income can be considerable.

The analysis in Chapter 2 focuses on two things. First, it is important that the set of relative prices prevailing in the economy encourages the efficient use of the existing stock of human resources. People are assets – in fact a country's most valuable assets – and it is essential for human development that these assets be deployed sensibly. A defective incentive system can result in a waste of human resources and often, too, in a higher incidence of poverty and greater inequality in the distribution of income. Second, it is equally important that the set of relative prices encourages the growth of the stock of human resources. It is not enough to use existing resources wisely; we must also add to the existing resources through human capital formation. The set of incentives should thus be examined to determine whether or not it encourages the acquisition of skills and knowledge by all members of society, male and female, and whether it encourages the discovery and dissemination of new knowledge, for example by rewarding research and innovation.

The focus shifts in Chapter 3 from prices, incentives and opportunities to the allocation of public expenditure. It is argued that in many countries human development requires a radical change in the way government spending is viewed. The conventional classification of expenditure into capital construction and recurrent items is more than misleading; it is positively harmful. According to the conventional view, the purchase of a physical asset, e.g. a school building, is regarded as capital accumulation which *ipso facto* contributes to growth and development, whereas the payment of salaries, e.g. to teachers, is regarded as recurrent expenditure which has no impact on growth and development. In fact, of course, depending on circumstances, the hiring of additional teachers may contribute more to development than the construction of additional school buildings. Thus governments which pursue a human development strategy will have to abandon old ways of thinking (which divide expenditure into public investment and public consumption) and adopt new ways based on new categories.

We also argue that a human development strategy frequently will entail a change in the sectoral composition of government expenditure and, in particular, a reallocation away from ministries concerned with 'production' (industry, agriculture, commerce) and 'law and order' (interior, defence) in favour of ministries concerned with the 'social services' (education, health, labour). Again it is misleading to think of spending on education, health, occupational safety, maternal care, etc., as social services; rather they should be seen as contributing to human capital formation. Similarly, much spending by the so-called production ministries has relatively little to do with increasing output but, instead, through subsidy policies, affects the distribution of income, often to the disadvantage of the poor.

Finally in Chapter 3 we argue that in many countries the process of human development would be accelerated by a reallocation of spending within the ministries concerned with human capital formation. Most of the available evidence indicates that when all costs and benefits are taken into account, the return on investment is higher at the base of a 'pyramid of expenditure' than at the summit. Thus the return on primary education is higher than the return on secondary education, which in turn is higher than the return on university education. Similarly, the return on expenditure on primary health care and preventive medicine is higher than the return on investments in hospitals and curative medicine. Again, the return on basic vocational training and apprenticeship programmes is higher than the return on expenditures intended to produce lawyers, highly-qualified business managers and certified public accountants.

There is thus a predisposition within a human development strategy to spread government spending evenly at the base of a pyramid of expenditure, to favour small projects rather than large, to disperse expenditure widely over a geographical area and to encourage local participation in programme implementation. These features of a human development strategy have the added advantages of tackling poverty directly (rather than relying on the benefits of growth to trickle down) and of confronting head-on major inequalities in education, health and training opportunities. Unfortunately, however, the actual pattern of public expenditure often is the opposite of that required by a human development strategy – spending is concentrated at the summit of an expenditure pyramid, large and prestigious projects are favoured, investment is geographically centralised (often in the capital) and popular participation is discouraged, obstructed and even suppressed.

Chapter 4 contains a short discussion of how policymakers should determine the size of human development expenditure programmes. The conventional approach of setting targets is contrasted with the recommended approach of a calculus of benefits and costs.

In Chapter 5 we discuss structural reforms, i.e. changes in institutions, property rights and entitlements that can have major effects on human development, the incidence of poverty and the distribution of wealth and income. Precisely because their effects are so penetrating, however, structural reforms usually are politically highly controversial and often are resisted by those who gain most from the *status quo*. None the less, in many countries structural reforms are fundamental to the success of a human development strategy. It is not enough to improve the set of incentives and alter the allocation of public sector resources; it is also necessary to create an institutional framework which guarantees to everyone gainful employment, access to productive assets and sufficient food to lead a healthy and well-nourished life. The poor should also be guaranteed a minimum of economic security.

There are, of course, several ways these objectives can be achieved and the specific programmes presented in Chapter 5 are intended to be illustrative: to show what has been tried, what works and what problems have been encountered. As in Chapter 3, the reader is asked in Chapter 5 to abandon old ways of thinking. We are not concerned with 'welfare' programmes as found in the welfare states of western Europe and North America, nor are we concerned with 'relief' programmes intended to alleviate temporary distress, as in the poor relief programmes of nineteenth-century Europe, the Civilian Conservation Corps of the 1930s depression in the United States and the famine-relief employment schemes of South Asia; nor, finally, are we concerned with purely redistributive measures intended to reduce inequality, such as progressive income taxation or means-tested benefits. We are concerned instead with reforms that promote human development, that is, structural reforms that increase the capabilities of people directly or that increase the pace of human capital formation and hence the capabilities of people in future. Old policies and programmes may look rather different when seen in this new light.

In Chapter 6 we turn to the relationship between human development and sustainable development. We argue that the two are highly compatible and that in fact sustainable development should be interpreted to mean a permanent, sustained increase in human capabilities. This in turn requires that the stock of total capital (natural, physical and human) be non-decreasing so that the flow of benefits in the form of capabilities remains unimpaired.

Lastly, in Chapter 7, we return to the question of financing human development. As should by now be clear, human development should not be used by the state as a justification for adding more to an existing framework – that is, for spending more and taxing more. Rather, human development should be interpreted as requiring the state to do something different. The reallocation of public sector resources implicit in this approach need not be accompanied by an expansion in the general level of government expenditure, although in some cases this may well be desirable. By and large, however, human development puts no higher burden on the public exchequer than alternative strategies of development. Moreover, the productivity of development expenditure is likely to be higher under a human development strategy than under other alternatives. The reason for this is that human development strategies channel resources to investment activities that are relatively neglected by other strategies but which enjoy above-average rates of return when all costs and benefits are properly measured. Thus a well-designed human development strategy should result in rates of growth of average income that are at least as high as could be achieved under a different strategy, and it should also result in a lower incidence of poverty and a greater degree of equality.

We are suggesting, in other words, that in the circumstances in which large numbers of developing countries find themselves there is unlikely to be a conflict between faster growth and greater equity in the distribution of the benefits of growth. This may not be true in all countries, however, or in all periods of history, and hence a brief word or two on possible 'trade-offs' may be useful. First, there may be a conflict between increasing output, or the rate of growth as conventionally measured, and increasing human development, i.e. raising the capabilities of people. Since conventional growth of output is solely a means to development, whereas increasing capabilities is the objective of development, if a conflict were to arise, the obvious choice is to sacrifice conventional growth in favour of human development. Second, there may be a conflict between raising the average level of human development (say, as measured by the human development index)[1] and achieving a more equal distribution of capabilities among the entire population. Here the conflict would have to be resolved by introducing value judgements about the degree of equality to which the society in question aspires. In principle, the human development index can be adjusted to reflect these normative preferences by incorporating distributional weights (e.g. for gender, ethnic groups, regions or the distribution of personal income), but it would be foolish to pretend that in practice it will be easy or even possible for policymakers to discover or create a consensus about the desired degree of equality. Finally, there may be a conflict between raising the average level of human development and reducing poverty, where the latter is regarded as an absolute concept. If such a conflict were to arise, then here again, value judgements would have to be introduced to resolve it. The interests of the poor, however, would almost always be better served by favouring a direct attack on poverty, even if this resulted in slower growth of conventional output or a slower average pace of human development or even, in some cases, in a fall in the average level of income per head. The indirect effects on poverty from a trickle-down of the benefits of growth seldom are sufficiently large or occur sufficiently fast to outweigh the direct benefits of redistributive policies. These three potential trade-offs, however, are rather hypothetical and, in most countries, one can be fairly confident that a human development strategy would not be in conflict with diminished poverty, greater equity or growth as conventionally measured.

Finally, human development strategies are likely to be less intensive in the use of foreign aid than more conventional alternatives. The reason for this is that human development strategies require less imported capital equipment than do alternative strategies and, in general, have lower demands for foreign exchange. Given that foreign finance is likely to be less readily available in the future than it was in the past, this characteristic of human development is to be welcomed. Developing countries, whether they like it or not, will be forced by circumstances to become more self-reliant, less dependent on foreign assistance. Those countries that choose a human development strategy will find themselves in the happy situation of having changed a necessity into a virtue and they will thereby enjoy an added bonus.

The strategy also has implications for foreign trade. Developing countries which adopt a human development strategy are likely to find that the basis of their comparative advantage in international trade shifts in favour of economic activities which use human capital relatively more intensively. Such countries will become inserted into the rapidly evolving global economy in a highly advantageous way, able to compete on equal terms with other nations while avoiding both the welfare-reducing protectionism of import-substituting industrialisation and the vulnerability to external shocks associated with specialisation on primary commodity exports.

1 The Essential Features of a Human Development Strategy

Human development is the ultimate objective of economic development. It is also a means – we shall argue, the best means available – for promoting development. Viewed as an end in itself rather than a means, human development is about enriching human lives. Material enrichment – producing a larger volume of goods and services – may contribute to this but it is not the same thing. Indeed it is by now widely understood that there is no one-to-one correspondence between material enrichment (measured, say, by gross national product per head) and the enrichment of human lives (measured, say, by the human development index). The human development approach thus implies the dethronement of national product as the primary indicator of the level of development.

The objective of development is not to produce more 'stuff', more goods and services, but, rather, to increase the capabilities of people to lead full, productive, satisfying lives.[1] A larger volume of output per head of the population may of course increase the capabilities of people, and thus should be warmly welcomed, but increased output should be seen for what it is: namely, an intermediate product that under appropriate circumstances can enhance human wellbeing. We should not lose sight of the fact that what ultimately concerns us is the ability of people to lead a long life (as measured perhaps by life expectancy at birth), to enjoy good health (as measured perhaps by morbidity rates), to have access to the stock of accumulated knowledge (as approximated by enrolment and literacy rates), to have sufficient income to buy food, clothing and shelter, to participate in the decisions that directly affect their lives and their community, and so on.

In formulating development policies, programmes and plans it is important to put people first, to specify objectives in terms of the enhancement of human capabilities. The more disaggregated are programme and policy objectives, the better. In addition to disaggregation by capabilities, at a minimum one should also disaggregate by occupational group and social class, gender and region and distinguish between rural and urban areas. In some countries, it might also be useful to classify people into separate

1

ethnic, religious or language groups. The appropriate categories for disaggregation will, of course, vary from one country to another depending on culture and history and the extent of social stratification.

The human development approach does not replace one aggregate statistic (GNP) by another (HDI) and then seek to maximise the numerical value of the replacement. Rather it views the objective of development as inherently multi-dimensional. There are numerous constituents of a person's (or a society's) wellbeing and, in assessing progress towards development, it is necessary to assess the constituent elements. This approach puts new and heavy demands on the statistical services – new, because most statistical bureaus have concentrated their efforts on collecting production, expenditure and income data for the conventional national accounting framework, and heavy, because the desired degree of disaggregation implied by the alternative framework is high – but the fact, where it is a fact, that human development cannot at present be accurately measured, need not prevent a country from adopting human development as a strategy for development.

HUMAN DEVELOPMENT AS A MEANS

The economic benefits received by people – whether in the form of money income, material goods and services received in kind, self-produced items of consumption or production, or capabilities such as a long life and good health which may be only partially mediated by relations of production and exchange – can be understood as flows originating from the stock of capital. The stock of capital, in turn, can be divided into three components: (i) the stock of natural capital, (ii) the stock of manmade physical capital and (iii) the stock of human capital.[2]

The stock of natural capital consists of the natural resources of the globe, including the atmosphere and oceans, the flora and fauna, the soils and mineral deposits and sources of fresh water. The stock of natural capital can be consumed (as when species become extinct), degraded (as when groundwater supplies are polluted by agricultural chemicals), maintained at a constant level of productivity (for example, by soil conservation) or augmented (for example, by tree-planting programmes). The stock of natural capital can also be transformed into physical capital, as when raw materials are combined to produce intermediate goods such as steel and electricity and capital goods such as machine tools and factory buildings.

Much of environmental and resource economics is concerned with the use of the natural stock of capital, including instances (which unfortunately are numerous) when market forces fail to produce price signals which accurately reflect social costs and benefits. The literature on market failure, missing markets and the optimal discount rate addresses some of the most important issues in environmental economics, issues which have become prominent in policy debates in both developing and developed countries in recent years.

The stock of physical capital consists of the produced means of production, i.e. the plant and equipment used in the agricultural, industrial and service sectors, the physical infrastructure (roads, bridges, ports, pipelines, railways, airports, irrigation canals) and the stock of dwellings. Just as natural capital can be consumed, degraded, maintained, augmented or transformed into other forms of capital, so too can physical capital. Much of traditional development economics in fact was primarily concerned with increasing the stock of physical capital, e.g. by creating incentives for businessmen to invest, by raising the savings rate or by establishing state-owned enterprises. Investment or the accumulation of capital – by which was meant the accumulation of physical capital – was for a long-time regarded as the engine of growth and development.

The stock of human capital consists of the knowledge, skills, experience, energy and inventiveness of people. It is acquired in a variety of ways: through training and apprenticeship programmes; while on the job through learning by doing; in the formal education system; through informal contacts by word of mouth; through newspapers, radio and the information media generally; in institutions devoted to pure and applied research; and through private study and reflection. The stock of human capital, like the stocks of physical and natural capital, will deteriorate if it is not maintained. Hence the importance of pre-natal and maternal care, school feeding and other nutrition programmes, the provision of safe drinking water, public health and disease-control measures, guaranteed employment schemes, and the like.

It is now recognised that human capital plays a central role in the development process and this has heightened interest in the economics of education, health economics, labour economics and related sub-disciplines. It is important to note, however, that human capital is just one component in the stock of total capital. Potential output and incomes rise when the stock of total capital increases, and in principle this could take place through net additions to the stocks of either natural, physical or human capital, or some combination of the three. It is important, of course, that the total stock of capital be utilised efficiently, given the state of technology, for technology, whether embodied in physical capital or in the knowledge possessed by human beings, is a powerful motor of growth in its own right. Ideally, expenditures should be allocated where returns are highest so that ultimately the returns on the margin are the same whether investment is in human, physical or natural capital. This will require constructing a calculus of benefits and costs, and devising methods that will enable reasonably accurate estimates to be made of all costs and all benefits associated with expenditure projects.[3] Meanwhile, there is a strong presumption that, under conventional development strategies, the *costs* associated with investments in natural capital have been greatly underestimated (partly because air, water and noise pollution and other negative externalities have been ignored),[4] while the *benefits* of investments in human capital have been underestimated. This has resulted in a pronounced bias against human capital expenditures, in favour of investments in physical capital and exploitation of natural resources.

A distinctive feature of a human development strategy is the emphasis placed on human capital formation. This does not mean that additions to the stocks of natural and physical capital are ignored – that would be a serious error – but it does mean a major change in priorities in favour of human capital. The justification for this change in priorities is, first, that the returns on investing in people are in general as high as, if not higher than, the returns to other forms of investment; second, that investment in human capital in some cases economises on the use of physical capital and the exploitation of natural resources; and third, the benefits of investing in people are in general more evenly spread than the benefits from other forms of investment. Thus a greater emphasis on human capital formation should result in as fast and perhaps even a faster pace of development, more sustainable development and a more equitable distribution of the benefits of development.

Of course, what is true of countries in general is not necessarily true of every particular country. In the absence of relevant country-specific data, policymakers may be forced to rely on comparative data from other countries, at least in the early stages of policy formulation; but it obviously would be better for each country to collect the information necessary to estimate the rates of return on various types of investment and to calculate the distributive implications of alternative investment patterns. Suffice it to say here that the evidence from around the world is that those countries that have given high priority to human capital formation have performed relatively well in terms of growth, employment, reduced inequality in the distribution of income and the alleviation of poverty.[5]

A second distinctive feature of a human development strategy is the importance of complementarities among the various kinds of human capital expenditures.[6] For example, expenditure on primary health care services should result in better health for the poor. This in turn should increase the efficiency with which the body transforms calories into improved nutrition, thereby increasing the benefits of maternal and child nutrition programmes, school lunch programmes and public food-distribution schemes. Improved nutrition increases the ability of children to learn and is likely also to result in higher rates of attendance at school. There are thus strong complementarities among primary health care, nutrition and education expenditures.

Similarly, there are linkages between expenditures devoted to improving the health of women and the amount of education women receive, their fertility and their life expectancy. There are linkages between literacy programmes, formal education and the productivity of labour as well as between literacy and health. Whenever complementarities such as these occur, the components of expenditure programmes should not be viewed in isolation but rather as a single package. That is, whenever complementarities are present, the whole is greater than the sum of its parts.

There are also complementarities between investing in people and investing in physical capital. Human capital is, of course, a direct input into the productive process. For instance, frequent illness lowers the productivity of labour while on the job and reduces the number of days worked. Hence programmes which result in improved health are not only valuable in themselves (human development as an end), but also have a positive impact on output (human development as a means). Similarly, the more skilled is the labour force, the higher will be its productivity. Skilled labour can not only do things beyond the competence of unskilled labour; it is likely also to be able to work faster, with less supervision, with fewer errors and to produce goods and services of a higher quality.

The complementarity between human capital and physical capital arises from the nature of the production process. Machines require trained workers to operate them and trained mechanics to repair them. Modern, productive agriculture requires a literate agricultural labour force: workers who can read instructions on a fertiliser bag, absorb information contained in literature distributed by extension agents and understand the contents of a repair manual for agricultural equipment. Modern services (travel, finance, tourism) require numeracy: people who can make simple calculations quickly and accurately. A country that gives priority to physical capital while neglecting its human capital will soon discover that the returns to physical capital are lower than they need be. Finally, investment in people is necessary for technical change, which (in combination with human capital) is the driving force of economic growth. It is difficult to introduce improved methods of production, new ways of doing things and more complex and sophisticated products unless buyers, workers and consumers have sufficient training and education to enable them to understand the technology. Thus physical capital formation, the accumulation of human capital and technical change are closely interlinked.

In summary, a human development approach has numerous advantages. First, it contributes directly to the wellbeing of people. Second, it builds from a foundation of equality of opportunity. Third, it helps to create a more equal distribution of the benefits of development. Fourth, it enables the linkages between the various types of investment in people to be fully exploited and, fifth, it takes advantage of the complementarities between human and physical capital.

THE ROLE OF THE STATE

These advantages, great as they are, do not materialise automatically. One institution, the state, must play a leading role in guiding the development process and intervening where necessary to ensure that the full benefits of human development are reaped. This does not imply that the state must be large in the sense of accounting for an unusually high proportion of total expenditure. Nor does this imply that the state should be relatively small, providing only minimal services and leaving the rest to the private sector. The size of the state is of secondary importance: what matters for human development is what functions the state performs, and how well it performs them.

Sri Lanka, for example, is widely known for giving high priority to human development expenditures, whereas Brazil has had different priorities and consequently a lower level of achievement. Central government expenditure in Brazil, however, was much higher than in Sri Lanka, namely, 36 per cent of gross national product in 1990 as compared to 28.4 per cent, respectively. Similarly, while average incomes are broadly comparable in Tunisia and Costa Rica, central government expenditure differs markedly, being 37.2 per cent of GNP in Tunisia and 27.1 per cent in Costa Rica. Yet Costa Rica's performance in terms of human development is much superior to Tunisia's. A large public sector with the wrong spending priorities, as in Brazil and Tunisia, will do little to promote human development, whereas a smaller public sector with better priorities, as in Costa Rica and Sri Lanka, can have a large impact on human development.

A second issue of limited relevance is the extent of decentralisation within the public administration. Many developing countries have highly centralised governments, often inherited from the colonial period, when the primary concern of the authorities was to maintain control over a subject population. After independence, the administrative structure frequently was retained with only minor modifications, even in countries where the size of the public sector increased dramatically and its range of functions widened considerably. The consequence was a sharp deterioration in the efficiency of public administration and a growing recognition that, regardless of the development strategy pursued, a less centralised bureaucracy was likely to be more effective. Thus a strong case for decentralisation can be made in many countries whether or not the country chooses to give high priority to human development. One should not push this argument too far, however. Indeed we shall argue in Chapter 5 that decentralisation is unlikely to be effective unless it includes devolution of power.

Admittedly the case for decentralisation gains added force when a human development strategy is adopted. The reason for this is that such a strategy tends to favour labour-intensive rather than capital-intensive projects, small and dispersed expenditures rather than large and geographically concentrated ones, and clusters of locally-based programmes which are complementary to one another, rather than homogeneous nationwide programmes. Central administrations located in capital cities are not well placed either to design or to implement development programmes with these characteristics. Put another way, human development strategies tend to be intensive in the use of local knowledge, and governments adopting such strategies are more likely to be successful when the public administration has strong ties to the grassroots.

This in turn implies the need to organise people around local institutions so that they can actively participate in formulating and implementing development programmes. Participation is of course an end in itself and the empowerment of people – giving them the capability to act in furthering their own interests – should be a central objective of human development. Indeed, the centrality of grassroots participation is an essential feature of the strategy and one which distinguishes it from other approaches. This does not imply that democratic participation will happen automatically, since democratic decision-making is a learned skill, but grassroots organisations do provide ideal vehicles for acquiring such skills. Human development ultimately rests upon a vigorous civil society – a host of non-governmental organisations that give people a voice and instruments for action – and in countries where civil society is weak, it should be a major purpose of public policy to invigorate it. The degree of decentralisation of the public administration, while important, is a secondary matter.

Quite apart from being an end in itself, participation has considerable instrumental value in a human development strategy. First, participation in representative grassroots organisations can make it easier to identify local opportunities for profitable expenditure and to specify priorities, identifying which projects are of primary importance and which can be postponed until additional resources become available. In other words, representative community-based institutions can help to define the content of development programmes at the local level and ensure that they accurately reflect local needs, aspirations and demands. Second, having helped to determine priorities and design development programmes, participation in functional organisations (irrigation societies, land reform committees, trade unions, women's groups, cooperatives) can then be helpful in generating support for national as well as local projects, programmes and policies. It is not sufficient for policymakers to be able to show that human development expenditures enjoy high returns; they must also show that there is sustained political support for such programmes from those who benefit from them.

Finally, participation is a valuable component of a development strategy because it can help to reduce the cost of public services and investment projects by shifting responsibility from central and local government (where costs tend to be relatively high) to the grassroots organisations (where costs tend to be relatively low). We shall argue below, for instance, that in some countries it may be possible to organise the beneficiaries of an investment project and persuade them to contribute their labour voluntarily to help defray some of the construction costs. This can occur, of course, only when the labourers do indeed become the principal beneficiaries of the completed project and this in turn may require that they become the owners of the assets they construct. In other cases some of the public services with a direct impact on human development (primary health care centres, nursery schools, food distribution points) can be organised, staffed and managed by local groups rather than by relatively highly-paid civil servants brought in from outside the community. If the benefits of a particular service can be limited to an identifiable group – a village, urban neighbourhood, lactating mothers – it may be possible to organise the group so that its members bear at least part of the cost of supplying the service. In these ways participation can be both an end and a means of human development.

CREATING A COALITION TO SUPPORT HUMAN DEVELOPMENT

As we have seen, human development is partly about the empowerment of people. Interventions by government to change relative prices in favour of human development, elimination of discrimination against women, the creation of additional employment opportunities, the removal of barriers inhibiting the expansion of the informal sector, greater access of small business to formal credit institutions, a reallocation of public sector resources to support human capital formation, and structural reforms favouring greater equity, food security and a general reduction in insecurity: all these policy changes will alter the distribution of income, wealth and political power. Those who lose from these changes, relatively and absolutely, can be expected to resist them. Since the losers are likely to be those who have prospered under the *status quo*, they are unlikely to be the uneducated, the undernourished, the unemployed, the unprivileged and the poor. On the contrary, the losers are likely to consist largely of the educated, articulate, organised middle and upper classes. Their political influence almost certainly will be considerable and should not be underestimated; they have the capacity to block policies promoting human development or to transmute such policies into programmes which support their interests. Government allocations favouring higher education, middle-class housing and urban hospitals are evidence of the ability of the powerful to control the public sector for their own ends.

The success of a human development strategy is thus likely to be contingent upon the political support of those who expect to gain from the change in strategy. The more numerous are the beneficiaries and the stronger are their organisations, the more likely it is that they will be able to overcome the resistance of those opposing change. It is not enough to design programmes which, if implemented, will increase the wellbeing of the great majority of people; it is also necessary to create the political conditions which make it possible actually to implement human development policies. Thus policymakers intending to introduce a human development strategy cannot afford to neglect the need to create a supporting coalition.

This coalition may or may not be based partly on political parties, but even if it is, support from other organised groups will be needed as well. Indeed, the points made above about the desirability of a vigorous civil society apply here too. Grassroots participation plays three roles: it is an end in itself, an instrument for increasing the productive potential of an economy and a means for generating and sustaining political support for human development. Locally-based non-governmental organisations give hitherto unorganised people a voice, an opportunity to articulate their needs and preferences, their vision of a better society. Policymakers should view them not as hostile to government or in conflict with its objectives but as an essential feature of a human development strategy.

2 The Structure of Incentives

The structure of incentives in an economy has a pervasive influence on the pace and pattern of development. Public expenditure is, of course, important, and in some cases decisive, but in the great majority of developing countries the public sector employs directly only a small fraction of the labour force and produces substantially less than half of all goods and services in the economy. Most people obtain their livelihood in the private sector, and most goods and services originate there. What is produced, how much is produced and what methods of production are used are questions decided largely in the private sector and primarily in response to the set of incentives which the private sector faces. The set of incentives, in turn, is strongly influenced by public policy, both directly and indirectly, and hence in formulating a human development strategy a good place to begin is by examining the structure of incentives.

It is often assumed that the structure of incentives in an economy can be fully described by the set of relative prices that prevails, and some economists reduce the incentives issue to exhortations about 'getting prices right'. The view taken here, however, is that prices constitute only a part, albeit an important part, of the structure of incentives. Equally important are barriers which exclude people from participating in some markets, as happens with licensing regulations; or features of an economy which restrict the ease of access of some people to markets, such as the restricted access of small businesses to formal sector credit markets; or overt discrimination, which reduces occupational mobility and income-enhancing opportunities of some people because of their racial, ethnic, gender or other characteristics, such as the customary discrimination against 'Untouchables' in India. Also important are cases of missing markets, where economic activity occurs without market mediation and consequently the output that is produced is not explicitly valued. An important example is labour performed by females within a household economy.

Thus the structure of incentives includes all activities, whether mediated by the market or not. And in the case of market-mediated activities, it includes discrimination, barriers to entry, market access and, of course, relative prices. The non-price aspects of the incentive system often are overlooked, yet as we shall see, they can have very large implications for human development.

11

EMPLOYMENT AND THE LABOUR MARKET

Women account for approximately half of the population, yet in the developing countries as a whole they represent less than a third of the labour force. In many countries the majority of women of working age are not classified as being in the labour force, i.e. according to official statistics they are not performing useful work. This, of course, is nonsense. The 'missing' female workers are engaged in a multiplicity of tasks – nurturing infants, educating pre-school children, caring for the sick, collecting water and fuel, preparing meals, managing the household. What distinguishes these activities from others is that the persons performing the work (women) are unpaid and the output produced (goods and services consumed within the household) is not valued by the market. We have here a massive instance of missing markets.

Because of the statistical invisibility of much work performed by women, many human development projects with potentially high returns fail to be implemented. These include projects which economise on the time of women and thereby reduce costs, as well as projects which enable women to produce more in a given period of time and thereby raise total output. Examples include investments in village water supplies (which save time spent fetching water), in fuel-efficient stoves (which save time collecting wood), in schooling for girls (which ultimately raises the productivity of women workers and reduces fertility rates) and in nutrition programmes (which improves the health and ultimately the productivity of all members of the household). The present structure of incentives is strongly biased against investment in these and similar areas, and governments wishing to promote human development would do well to bring under the calculus of benefits and costs the many activities undertaken where markets are missing.

Apart from unpaid women producing unpriced goods and services, there are also women classified as being economically active, i.e. as being members of the labour force, but who receive no remuneration for their work. The most important example is in agriculture. In some parts of the world, especially in sub-Saharan Africa, women supply most of the labour used to grow food crops. The output of women's labour (cereals, pulses, vegetables, root crops) may well be valued by the market even when most of the production is for consumption within the household, but the labour of the women may not be valued by the market because, for example, it is applied to land owned by the male head of household or tenanted by the male head of household. The structure of incentives in this case may not be biased against the crops grown by women but it is biased against innovations which reduce the time and effort spent by women in cultivation, since the labour of women is treated as if it had no cost. Thus the returns on investments in improved hand implements used by women are overlooked, as are possibilities for substituting draft animal power for digging sticks, improved harvesting methods, better storage and food-processing techniques, etc.

Where the structure of incentives treats the labour of women as a free good, women become an 'invisible input' in the process of production. This phenomenon is widespread and has led to a pattern of development expenditure that is neither efficient nor equitable. Once again, governments wishing to promote human development would do well to recognise the full implications of the missing market for female labour.

Not infrequently labour markets are characterised not only by missing markets but also by obvious discrimination. The basis of discrimination can be almost anything – gender, race, ethnicity, language, religion, citizenship – and seems to be limited only by the imagination of humankind in devising plausible criteria for distinguishing one group from another. Discrimination need not, of course, be restricted to the labour market and, in fact, economic discrimination often is reinforced by discrimination in the political and social spheres of life. In the economic sphere with which we are here concerned, however, discrimination can be understood to serve two purposes: to reserve certain well-paid, highly desirable occupations to a privileged minority and to confine certain groups to low-paid, undesired occupations. That is, discrimination reduces the upward occupational mobility of the unprivileged groups, increases competition among them for the jobs for which they are eligible, and thereby increases the supply of workers at the lower end of the job ladder and reduces the wage rate. At the top end of the job ladder, discrimination reduces the supply of competing labour, restricts competition and raises the wage rate.

The most elaborate system of discrimination is that of rural India, where occupational segregation is intimately connected to the caste hierarchy. Elsewhere discrimination may be based on race, as in South Africa, where blacks are largely restricted to mining, agricultural labour and low-skilled jobs in urban areas. Even in Brazil, where overt discrimination is illegal, informal discrimination is widespread and there is a close correlation between skin colour and rungs on the job ladder, with black-skinned persons on the lowest rungs and light-skinned persons on the highest. In parts of East Africa and Southeast Asia, discrimination is based on ethnic origin, with persons of south Asian origin being discriminated against in East

Africa and persons of Chinese origin being discriminated against in South-east Asia.

Discrimination, of course, restricts choice and reduces opportunities; it makes it difficult and sometimes impossible for people to enlarge their capabilities and achieve their full potential. It is thus antithetical to the goals of human development. More subtle than overt discrimination are barriers to entry into certain occupations. In Andean America, for instance, those who speak an indigenous language (Aymara, Quechua) and wear native costume find it difficult to enter relatively well-paid urban occupations or to obtain jobs in the public administration; they are effectively confined to the rural areas and to the informal urban sector. European dress and a know-ledge of Spanish are used as barriers to entry into formal sector occupations, and the language barrier in particular can be quite formidable when low public expenditure on primary and secondary education in the countryside leads to low enrolment rates among the children of indigenous peoples.

Many occupations are in practice reserved for men – politics, the legal profession, senior positions in the public administration, the police and armed forces – and even when formal barriers to entry are absent, women often encounter 'glass ceilings' which prevent them climbing to the top of the job ladder. Formal sector employment for women often is limited to filing clerks, shop attendants and domestic service and in countries where competition for urban jobs is especially keen, as in south Asia, even these sources of employment are reserved for men. The gender division of labour sometimes is defended on grounds that it reflects the culture of a particular country, but when women are denied choice, opportunity and avenues to enlarge their capabilities, 'culture' should be seen not as a distinctive and valuable mark of civilisation, but as ideology sanctioning barriers to the human development of women.

The price component of the structure of labour market incentives, i.e. the set of relative wage rates, has received much attention. The thrust of the argument is that, in general, wage rates in the urban formal sector have been too high in the sense that the cost of labour to employers has exceeded its opportunity cost, i.e. the value of the output produced by the next best alternative use of labour. Many reasons have been advanced for the rela-tively high cost of formal sector labour: the wage policies adopted by the government itself for public sector employees, minimum wage legislation, the ability of labour unions to push wages above a market clearing level, etc. There is little doubt that, in many occupational categories, there is an excess supply of labour at the going wage rate, although the belief that these wages are inflexible downwards has been undermined by the sharp fall in real wages that occurred in the formal sector in East Africa during the severe economic crises of the 1980s.[1]

Whenever there is an excess supply of people seeking work at the going wage rate, there is at least a suspicion that employment opportunities could be increased, and human development thereby promoted, by lowering formal sector wages. This apparently simple remedy is more complex than first appears, however. Whether some wages are 'too high', even non-market clearing wages, depends on the context and the forces operating in the various labour markets. We have shown that the labour 'market' in developing countries is highly fragmented. In some cases markets are missing; in others there are numerous barriers to entry; in still others there is covert or overt discrimination. In addition, labour markets are segmented, with workers in the urban informal sector and rural occupations receiving very low remuneration and workers in the urban formal sector usually enjoying relatively high wages. These high wages, in turn, often are a result of decisions by firms to pay wages above the market clearing level to reduce turnover or, as we have seen, they are a direct result of government policy.

These fragmented and segmented labour markets should be seen as a whole, as a system of labour control. The structure of incentives within this system restricts the occupational and social mobility of a large portion of the population: it keeps people, men and women, 'in their place'. At the same time, it sometimes produces relatively high incomes for a very small but privileged minority of the labour force. That is, the structure of incentives leads simultaneously to an inefficient use of labour and an unequal distribution of income. Thus the issue confronting those who wish to promote human development is not that the price of formal sector labour is too high (i.e. above its opportunity cost), but that the structure of the labour market operates in such a way that a disproportionately large fraction of the labour force is compelled to seek a livelihood at the bottom of the occupational hierarchy, with the result that the remuneration of most workers is lower than it otherwise would be and in some cases (particularly for women) is zero. The policy implication is not to raise or lower a particular wage or set of wages but to reform the system of labour control.

None of this should be taken to imply, however, that a highly 'fluid' labour market, with high turnover and little sense of loyalty or commitment between employer and employee, is preferable to a more 'rigid' labour market in which formal sector workers enjoy security of employment. A combination of relatively high wages (to reduce labour turnover) and job security (to encourage workers to invest in firm specific human capital and to cooperate in the introduction of technical innovation), as in Japan, may actually be more efficient in the long run than labour markets which conform to the textbook descriptions of perfect competition.[2]

ACCESS TO FINANCE CAPITAL

Many of the issues that arise in trying to understand the structure of incentives in the labour market also arise when studying the capital market. In many developing countries the most prominent feature of the capital market is its structural dualism, i.e. its division in two parts, a formal and an informal sector. The formal financial sector contains commercial banks, insurance companies, perhaps a stock market, a government-established and -operated development bank, and perhaps a housing finance institution. These institutions cater to the needs of large, well-established industrial and service enterprises (domestic and foreign), the wealthy (for personal loans), the upper middle class (in the case of mortgages) and, in the rural areas, large farmers, ranchers and plantation companies. The informal credit market – the black, grey and curb markets – consists of pawn shops, money-changers operating on city sidewalks, professional rural moneylenders, shopkeepers who also provide credit for their trusted customers, large landowners who provide credit for their tenants, and friends and relatives who occasionally come to the rescue of those in distress. The informal credit market thus serves the majority of the population: small businesses in general, the urban informal sector, peasant farmers, the poor.

The formal credit market differs from the informal credit market in terms of price and ease of access. Prices charged in the formal credit market are relatively low. Nominal rates of interest are modest, sometimes below the rate of inflation, and consequently real rates of interest may even be negative. The low cost of credit to borrowers leads to enormous excess demand in the market and hence severe credit rationing. Those who succeed in obtaining cheap credit, however, have a strong incentive to invest in mechanised techniques of production, i.e. to economise on the use of labour and human capital generally. The result is an inefficient allocation of finance capital (an excessive degree of mechanisation) combined with an unequal distribution of income (because the chosen factor proportions shift value-added away from wages towards profits and rents).

The rate of interest in the informal credit market varies over an enormous range. In some cases it is zero (e.g. occasional loans among relatives); in other cases real rates of interest can be extremely high (e.g. seasonal credit supplied by moneylenders to small landowning peasant cultivators); while in other cases the rate of interest is indeterminate (as when factor markets are interlinked and landowners, say, offer their tenants a 'package' of land use, credit and marketing services in return for a share of the crop intended to cover rent, interest and transport costs).[3] In general, however, the cost of credit in the informal capital market is a multiple of the cost in the formal capital market and this provides a strong incentive for borrowers to adopt excessively labour-intensive methods of production, with the result that the productivity of labour, and hence labour incomes, are lower than they would otherwise be. That is, incentives generated in the formal credit market encourage borrowers to reduce the employment of labour, whereas incentives generated in the informal credit market force borrowers to adopt techniques which reduce the productivity of labour and the earnings of working people, including the self-employed. In both cases the set of incentives is inimical to human development.

This outcome arises from persistent differences in ease of access of different groups of people to the formal and informal credit markets. If the two markets were closely integrated, discrepancies in interest rates and in the cost of capital in general would be reduced by arbitrage to differences in risk, transaction costs and the cost to lenders of acquiring information. Actual differences in the cost of capital between the informal and formal credit markets, however, are much greater than can be justified by risk premia and the costs of doing business. The differences are so great because the degree of integration is low; for practical purposes, the two markets are virtually separate.

Illiterate farmers, self-employed itinerant vendors, fishermen, rural artisans, small shopkeepers, urban informal sector producers and workers, small businessmen engaged in urban or inter-provincial transport, and women in general have little or no access to the commercial banking system. They are forced to rely on the informal credit market and many persons are unable to obtain credit even from that source. They are excluded by their inability to read and write, by unfamiliarity with administrative procedures, by lack of collateral and by insecure legal titles to their property.

A human development strategy should seek to improve access to credit markets not by passing so-called anti-usury laws but by increasing the supply of credit channelled through the informal credit markets and by changing the characteristics of informal sector borrowers so they become more creditworthy. Anti-usury laws directed at moneylenders and other informal sector suppliers of credit, far from lowering interest rates, will instead reduce the supply of credit, raise costs of lending and actually push up informal sector interest rates. Such legislation will only make matters worse. Instead the government should work with the informal sector lenders, channelling funds through informal sector institutions in order to increase the availability of credit and lower its cost. There is no need, however, for the government to go to the opposite extreme and subsidise credit by lending at artificially low interest rates.

In some societies women have particular difficulties in obtaining loans for small-scale economic activities, partly because they are not allowed to own, or in practice do not possess, property that can be used as collateral. In many parts of the world, but particularly in Africa, women have attempted to overcome discrimination against them in the credit market by forming rotating savings and credit associations or other cooperative arrangements.[4] In other cases banks have been formed which combine small loans and technical assistance to women, the loans being secured by the commitment of a group of women to assume responsibility for each other's debts. The most famous example is the Grameen Bank in Bangladesh.[5] Government support for such initiatives can go part of the way toward increasing the supply of credit in informal capital markets.

Access to credit can be improved through increased literacy (which enables borrowers to enter into formal loan contracts), by expenditure on primary and secondary education in rural areas (which builds self-confidence and familiarity with routine administrative formalities) and by providing secure titles to land and other assets. In many developing countries, especially in Latin America and parts of Southeast Asia, private land tenure is insecure. This affects small cultivators in particular and, notably, those on the margins of the cultivated area who have cleared forests to bring more land under the plough. Adjudication of ownership claims often takes years and meanwhile property rights are insecure. This, in turn, has three effects. First, insecurity of tenure discourages long-term investment in immovable assets. It creates a disincentive to increase the stock of natural capital – land improvements, conservation measures – and to invest in certain types of complementary physical capital – fences, barns and other structures. Thus the set of incentives actually encourages environmental degradation.[6] Second, insecure titles reduce the price which land can fetch in the market, and this provides an incentive for the wealthy, who can afford the time and cost of adjudicating property claims, to purchase land from the poor at a discount. This then leads to increased inequality in the distribution of wealth. Third, insecurity makes it difficult for small farmers to raise credit from the commercial banks because formal sector lenders are reluctant to supply capital to those without clear titles.[7] Thus a weakness in the land market, namely insecure private tenure, raises a barrier to entry into the formal sector capital market.

Looking beyond capital markets to the distribution of investment opportunities, it is often assumed that one of the things that distinguishes the informal sector of the economy from the formal sector is an absence of barriers to entry. In the informal sector – characterised as it is by small, labour intensive enterprises, self-employment and low-skilled services – it is taken for granted that competition is intense and there is freedom of entry and exit. And at a certain level of analysis this description is undoubtedly correct. It is also the case, however, that informal sector enterprises often are prevented by law from competing with formal sector enterprises. A host of barriers to entry have been erected to protect the formal sector from competition from the informal sector. These barriers take the form of licences, regulations, city ordinances and other controls which exclude informal sector enterprises from profitable activities in urban transport (taxis, buses, minivans), construction and food services and regulate competition by sidewalk vendors with formal sector retail establishments. The ostensible reasons for these regulations and controls are the health, safety and convenience of the public, but given that most of the public are poor people who would benefit from the freedom to compete and seek a better livelihood in highly profitable, protected activities, it seems that the real reason lies elsewhere, in protecting the incomes of the relatively well-to-do.

Governments seeking to promote human development should reexamine their regulatory systems with a view to removing restraints on the growth and development of the informal sector. The structure of incentives faced by members of this sector tends to perpetuate poverty and inefficiency and to retard the overall rate of growth of the economy. Liberating the private sector could usefully begin by removing shackles which hobble the expansion and diversification of activities which potentially are attractive to people with only limited access to capital.[8]

LAND, NATURAL CAPITAL AND COMPARATIVE ADVANTAGE

We have concentrated so far on labour and capital markets and the various ways public policy could be used to improve the structure of incentives in support of human development. When designing a human development strategy, however, it is not enough to scrutinise labour and capital markets for possible malfunctioning; other markets should also be examined, particularly markets that supply widely-used inputs that influence the structure of costs in a variety of economic activities. The land market is a case in point.

We have already argued that insecure land titles contribute to the difficulties faced by small farmers in obtaining credit. The problems associated with land management and land use, however, go beyond the issue of private property rights. Publicly-owned land often has been managed inefficiently, has accentuated environmental degradation and has benefited disproportionately the upper-income groups. Encroachments on public lands (forests, grazing land, mountainous areas) is common. Because of poor management, public land often is treated as a free good; the resource base is 'mined' and environmental damage can be extensive; the 'tragedy of the commons' is the result. In Southeast Asia, timber pricing policies on public land have led to a waste of forest resources and a failure to replant.[9] In Brazil, government subsidies and tax incentives have led to extensive clearing of the Amazon forest. Indeed, the only way to obtain title to land in the Amazon is by removing the trees from the land.[10] Similar problems arise with respect to the use of publicly-owned subsurface water: it is often treated as a free good, is consequently used wastefully and the rate of extraction usually exceeds the recharge rate, thus ensuring that the process ultimately is unsustainable.

Heavy government expenditure on subsidies to fuel, chemicals and water has tilted incentives away from human capital in favour of intensive exploitation of natural capital. Fertiliser has been heavily subsidised in India and the other countries of south Asia with the result that surface water (rivers, lakes) and groundwater supplies have become polluted. Subsidies to pesticides (and also, to some extent, herbicides) have led to a concentration of toxic chemicals in water and land, and in a few instances this has threatened to reduce biological diversity. Subsidies to fuel have encouraged agricultural mechanisation at the expense of employment of labour. Perhaps most serious of all has been massive public investment in managed irrigation systems and the provision of water to farmers by the state at prices well below cost. In Egypt, irrigation water from the Nile is free; in Brazil and other parts of Latin America, the price of government-supplied irrigation water does not even cover the variable costs of the irrigation system, let alone the capital costs; the same is true of publicly-managed irrigation systems in North Africa, the Middle East and south Asia.

The set of incentives created by government intervention in market processes has had four unfortunate effects. First, it has damaged the environment and led to the depletion of the natural stock of capital through soil salination, deforestation, water pollution, etc. Second, as we will see in

Chapter 3, the government subsidies which underpin the set of incentives have absorbed a significant portion of the public revenues potentially available to support human development. The benefits of the subsidies have accrued not to the poor but primarily to upper-income groups. Third, the structure of incentives has led to an inefficient use of resources; it has sent false signals to producers and helped to entrap developing countries in a pattern of production which is economically disadvantageous. The structure of incentives has led countries to adopt the wrong comparative advantage, to concentrate on products which are overly intensive in the use of natural capital and to neglect their potential comparative advantage in products which are intensive in the use of human capital. As a result, the shift out of primary commodity exports has been slower than it might have been and the creation of new comparative advantages in skilled-labour-intensive manufactured products and services has been delayed. Finally, the structure of incentives has led not only to static inefficiency in resource allocation and a pattern of trade that fails to reflect long-run comparative advantage; it has also led to a pattern of investment that tends to perpetuate the *status quo*. That is, government subsidies to fuels, fertiliser, pesticides, water, timber and land affect not only the use of the existing stock of capital, whether natural, physical or human, they also generate political pressure from the beneficiaries of the subsidies for additional public investment in related areas (irrigation, state-owned fertiliser plants, highways to open up virgin forests) and for ever-larger subsidies to inputs. Once embarked on this road, it is difficult to change direction: vested interests can be expected to exert pressure to sustain existing programmes. Hence the need for reform-minded governments actively to build coalitions to support human development.

HUMAN CAPITAL AND DYNAMIC COMPARATIVE ADVANTAGE

As suggested in the previous paragraph, compared to conventional strategies, a human development strategy is more conducive to promoting the long-term comparative advantage of a developing country. Some developing countries may be endowed with an abundance of natural resources, but the costs associated with trying to exploit this comparative advantage for international trade have invariably been underestimated. When the true domestic opportunity costs of environmental degradation have been ascertained, many countries may not indeed be blessed with a real comparative advantage, certainly not at the rate at which they are exploiting their natural capital. Rather, their long-term comparative advantage may be better cultivated by investing in human capital. If the development policies of governments have not reflected such an orientation, one of the major reasons is that the benefits of investment in human capital have not been fully recognised.

During the 1980s many developing countries still relied heavily on the export of primary commodities and confronted sharply declining terms of trade for these products.[11] Those countries which succeeded in making the transition to exporting labour-intensive manufactures fared better. But even the terms of trade for manufactured exports began to show signs of decline.[12] This underlines the importance for developing countries of developing a long-run, dynamic view of their comparative advantage. If countries are to compete in a global economic environment undergoing dramatic change, driven in part by rapid technological innovation, it is essential that they continuously upgrade the skills and education of their workforce. For most countries this will require a significant reallocation of public sector resources towards programmes promoting human capital formation. One of the reasons that there is a low social rate of return on highly-skilled labour in developing countries is that employment sometimes is not available for many of the people who complete a tertiary education. While there may be deficient demand for scientists, engineers, computer specialists and other professionals now, if developing countries concentrate on enhancing their long-run comparative advantage, these skills will be in increasing demand in future.

Enhancing a country's long-run comparative advantage requires an activist state. This may not be a state which engages in large public investment projects, but it must be a state which attempts to influence the allocation of resources in the direction which best promotes the long-term growth and development of the economy. Especially with regard to human development expenditures, which are characterised by many positive externalities and complementarities, the private market mechanism tends to underallocate resources for such purposes. It is incumbent on the state to ensure that there is adequate financing for human capital formation, not only to increase present income flows, but also to ensure future high rates of growth.

If a developing country concentrates on human capital as the basis for its long-run comparative advantage, this does not imply that it should follow an export-promoting or export-biased trade strategy. An export-promoting strategy biases domestic output towards supplying external demand rather than domestic demand and thereby subjects a country to the fluctuations and uncertainties of the international market. This strategy could be risky during a period in which protectionism has been on the rise in developed countries, the rate of the growth of the global economy has been slowing, and potentially exclusionary trading blocs are emerging.

A more sensible policy is one which fosters an open economy, but open in the sense that it biases production neither towards exports nor towards domestic demand.[13] The exchange rate is not deliberately undervalued in order to boost exports artificially. Such a policy of undervaluation may enable a country to export a greater volume of labour-intensive manufactures based initially on its endowment of low-skilled labour, but it does not engender the competitive pressures that compel a country to make the transition to more human-capital-intensive exports. Indeed undervaluation works by depressing domestic real wages and redistributing income from wages to profits, particularly within the export sector. The export sector is then expected to act as an engine of growth for the entire economy.

Under an open economy trade regime neither is the exchange rate overvalued, since this would enable a country artificially to cheapen the import of capital and intermediate goods. Overvalued exchange rates have been characteristic of import substitution trade regimes. The policies of import substitution – overvalued exchange rates, high tariffs, physical import controls, restrictions on foreign exchange and capital movements, and cheap rationed financial capital – have fostered a capital-intensive structure of production in many developing countries and undermined their potential comparative advantage in labour-intensive exports. In general, the policies have biased investment towards physical capital and away from human capital. Pakistan represents a classic example of the distortions in resource allocation which result from import substitution policies.[14]

A trade orientation based on a comparative advantage arising from a relative abundance of human capital is not only likely to engender a more rapid rate of long-term growth than one based on physical capital or natural capital, but it is also likely to distribute the benefits of such growth more equitably. In most developing countries, ownership of land and other natural resources is unequally distributed, as is the ownership of physical capital. Exports intensive in the use of natural resources or physical capital mainly serve to enlarge the share of rents or profit in national income, whereas labour-intensive exports help to increase the share of wages.

TECHNOLOGICAL CAPABILITIES AND HUMAN DEVELOPMENT

The global distribution of technological capabilities is highly unequal, even more unequal than the global distribution of income or the global distribution of physical capital. Indeed, technological capabilities are highly concentrated even among the developed economies. Except for a handful of newly-industrialising countries, developing countries have few technological capabilities. Their initial task should be to create a broad base of scientific and technical knowledge among the population and build on this base so as to reduce gradually the gap between developed and developing countries. The policy we advocate, in other words, is to build from the ground up.

It would be misguided for developing countries to attempt to incorporate the most sophisticated technologies into their present structures of production. An attempt to do so would require massive expenditure on research and development, a commitment to produce large numbers of highly-trained scientists, engineers and technicians, and an entrepreneurial class capable of transforming scientific advances into commercially profitable activities. Even if such an attempt succeeded, it would warp the economy, accentuate inequality in the distribution of income and produce lower returns than alternative, less capital-intensive investments.

Within the developing countries there are strong arguments, on grounds of efficiency and equity, for placing primary emphasis on mass education as the way to increase technological capabilities. Conventional thinking visualises technological progress in idealist terms, as a series of dramatic breakthroughs made by an elite group of scientists and engineers. Careful study of the historical record, however, suggests that this vision is incorrect. Technological progress can better be understood as a long, gradual process, based on shop-floor improvements discovered or devised by ordinary technicians and workers while struggling to adapt new technology to their specific conditions. Often there is a smooth continuum from initial discovery of a scientific principle to development of its technical feasibility to transformation into a commercially viable innovation and finally to widespread diffusion of the technology. In the case of Watts' steam engine, for example, it took a full century after the initial development in the 1760s and 1770s, a century of design changes and gradual improvements, before this new source of power displaced the sail on ocean-going vessels and overtook water-power on land.[15]

An important aspect of the continuum of technological innovation is the process of learning and the development of the human skills necessary for introducing and diffusing a new technology. These 'learning-by-applying' efforts lie behind sustainable technological advances. They are the result not of chance or unpredictable brilliance but of a deliberate pattern of resource allocation: a pattern which favours not so much highly-educated researchers and well-equipped laboratories and research facilities as primary and secondary education and, above all, popular scientific and technical education. The skills produced by such a pattern of expenditure are the ultimate source of innovations. These skills, however, are acquired informal aptitudes, general predispositions which are not registered on standard rating measures of formal technological capacities.[16]

These informal aptitudes embrace 'learning-by-doing', minor improvements which are motivated by cost savings, enhanced maintenance, reverse engineering and 'learning-by-using'. As was pointed out in Kenneth Arrow's classic work on 'learning-by-doing', many incremental improvements in technology occur as by-products of workers and technicians discovering how to carry out production more efficiently.[17] Nathan Rosenberg's concept of 'learning-by-using' is similar, but includes a more explicit effort to understand the technology embodied in a product or a machine, often by taking it apart to identify its design.[18] Both 'learning-by-doing' and 'learning-by-using' are low-cost activities, and hence it should be possible for developing countries to increase their technological capabilities quickly by giving priority to mass scientific education.

Higher costs are associated with more advanced formal education or 'learning-through-training'. This involves some systematic instruction in the 'know-how' of technology but it does not necessarily include an understanding of the 'know-why' of technology or the basic principles of operation. Again, the historical evidence suggests that 'learning-through-training' was crucial to the success of those developing countries which became internationally competitive in exporting manufactured goods.

Still more advanced is 'learning-by-searching'. This refers to the ability to investigate the available technology and to choose what is most appropriate for a given country's stage of economic development.[19] If a country is able to engage in 'learning-by-searching', it must have a larger stock of scientists and engineers than countries pursuing a broader-based strategy and must devote a considerable volume of resources to research and development. Although 'learning-by-searching' is important and ultimately will be essential, most developing countries would not be well advised to give top priority to creating a high level of capacity to investigate and absorb foreign technology. The resources required to nurture a domestic scientific and engineering elite and to mount a major effort in R&D activities would be better used to provide education and training in scientific subjects for the majority of the country's labour force.

In most developing countries indigenous technological capabilities can be increased most efficiently by giving priority to constructing the foundations, i.e. by concentrating on basic human capital formation. Broad literacy and numeracy come first. Next come education in popular science and elementary technical training. The acquisition of these essential skills by a large proportion of the population is the surest way to promote sustainable and steady technological change. An emphasis on 'learning-by-applying' will ensure that a country is able to institutionalise continuous improvements in its technological capabilities. In the absence of this, even massive expenditure on educating scientists and engineers, hiring expatriate research personnel and on R&D will produce meagre results.

It takes many years to produce a stock of competent scientists and engineers. In Africa less than one per cent of the children entering primary school go on to study post-secondary science, engineering or technical subjects. The reason for this is that children in primary school are poorly educated in science and mathematics, and this weakness of the school system makes it difficult to improve technological capabilities. To produce a scientist or engineer normally requires five to ten years of education beyond secondary school, but in order to have a critical mass of students at the post-secondary level it is necessary to provide secondary school students with an adequate background in science and technology, and this in turn implies that the foundations at the primary level must be strong.[20] Alas, in many developing countries, not just in Africa, the foundations are weak. Indeed in most developing countries a strong emphasis on basic human capital formation is essential both to ensure broadly-based technical competence among the labour force and to produce an adequate number of scientists and engineers.

An emphasis on basic human capital formation also has the advantage that it helps to ensure that the fruits of technical change are widely distributed among the population. The alternative strategy, relying on an elite group of scientists and engineers, tends to increase the concentration of incomes. Again, the more broadly-based strategy of emphasising basic human capital formation is more likely to result in the adoption of technology that is appropriate to the country's existing structure of production and is designed to meet the basic needs of the population.

Indeed, if a human development strategy is pursued consistently, human capital will emerge as the main source of a country's comparative advantage in the long-run. It is often argued that the comparative advantage of developing countries in the international division of labour rests on their relative abundance of unskilled labour. In a static sense, at a given moment in time, this may be true, but in a dynamic sense human capital formation can shift a country's comparative advantage from labour as such to skill-enhanced labour. That is, as the stock of human capital increases and it becomes relatively more abundant, the composition of output will change in favour of more human-capital-intensive products. This will be accompanied by an increase in the productivity of labour and a rise in living standards. The long-term comparative advantage of developing countries that pursue a human development strategy will rest on technology embodied not so much in their stock of physical capital as in their human capital.

COMPLEMENTARITIES BETWEEN PUBLIC AND PRIVATE INVESTMENT

As we have seen, governments affect the set of incentives to which private producers respond and, because of the dynamics of the political process, state investment also is likely to respond to the set of government-influenced incentives. In principle, this is not undesirable. After all, if the set of incentives provides correct signals for resource allocation, it would be desirable for both the private and public sectors to respond to the same signals. If the signals are misleading, perhaps in the ways suggested above, this is an argument for changing the structure of incentives, not for reducing the level of government activity. That is, a defective set of incentives caused partly by government subsidies and other forms of intervention should not necessarily be interpreted as evidence of 'government failure' resulting from incompetence or ignorance; it might simply reflect a different set of policy goals.

Many cases can be found – Haiti is a glaring example – where governments have been prepared to sacrifice efficiency, protection of the environment, growth and poverty alleviation for higher incomes for their supporters. The structure of incentives necessary to achieve this result may be highly successful in its own terms and it would be a mistake to claim that in such cases public policy is prone to 'government failure' and future governments should abstain from interfering with the market. Moreover, even in genuine cases of government failure, it does not follow that the best solution is to reduce the scale of government activities. It might be more sensible to correct the failure, e.g. by increasing the information available to the government, by devoting resources to training programmes for civil servants, or by reforming the public administration to make it more accountable to the general public.

A human development strategy is likely to require an activist state. First, it will have to intervene to correct the bias in favour of products and processes of production which are intensive in the use of natural capital. If left to its own devices the market tends to ignore many costs which damage the environment. Second, it will have to intervene to correct the bias against human capital formation. If left to its own devices the market tends to ignore many of the benefits associated with expenditure on human development. Third, the state will have to be active in financing and undertaking investment broadly conceived, including expenditure on research and development, education and training, health and nutrition, as well as investment in many forms of physical capital such as transport, power and urban infrastructure.

It is sometimes claimed that public expenditure 'crowds out' private expenditure and that the returns on private investment are greater than the returns on public expenditure. This is then used as an argument to reduce taxation and state spending. In the case of a human development strategy, however, this argument clearly is wrong: public investment, broadly defined, is complementary to private investment. We have here a case of 'crowding in', not 'crowding out'.

Precisely because human development expenditures generate positive externalities – benefits that are not fully captured by the market mechanism – the state must take the lead in a wide range of activities from child nutrition programmes to investments in scientific research and technology. Once these state investments are in place, the private sector can appropriate the external benefits through investments of its own and, in so doing, obtain a higher rate of profit than would otherwise be possible. That is, the rate of profit on private investment varies positively with public expenditure on human development. At the same time, the benefits of public expenditure on human development are realised partly as a result of employment generated by private investment. Public and private investment thus are complementary to one another.[21] The larger the expenditure on human development, the larger is likely to be the volume of private investment. In addition, the larger the expenditure on human development, the more even will be the distribution of income, everything else being equal, and partly because of its effects on private investment, the faster will be the overall rate of growth.

SUMMARY

The structure of incentives refers not only to the set of relative prices that prevails in an economy but also to the degree of access to markets, barriers to entry and discrimination. In many developing countries the structure of incentives is in conflict with the objectives of human development and it will be important in designing a human development strategy to consider how best the structure of incentives can be improved.

Human development is much concerned with correcting market failures, particularly failures of factor markets. If left to its own devices, the signals generated by an unrestricted market would lead to systematic underinvestment in the stock of human capital, including expenditures on training and apprenticeship programmes, all three levels of formal education, basic health care, pre- and post-natal maternal and child care and nutrition programmes. All of these activities have some of the characteristics of 'public goods' and generate positive externalities. The market would also lead to underinvestment in research in science and technology – because private firms cannot capture the full benefits of their expenditure on research and development (despite patents and copyright laws), because investment in scientific research is 'lumpy' and characterised by economies of scale over a considerable range, and because individual research projects viewed in isolation are often risky and consequently unattractive unless pooled in a large national research programme.

Labour markets in developing countries often are far from efficient. They are highly fragmented and sometimes segmented into non-competing or only partially competing groups. Discrimination against women and other groups in society is common. There are many barriers to entry into high-paying occupations and access to formal sector employment is restricted. Wage rates fail to reflect the opportunity cost of labour, being too low at the lower end of the job hierarchy and too high at the top end. There is thus a strong case for a government committed to a human development strategy to become actively involved in improving the functioning of labour markets.

Broadly similar issues arise in the case of financial and capital markets. The price of finance capital in formal sector markets often is below the opportunity cost of capital, thereby discouraging investment in human capital and the creation of formal sector employment. In the informal sector, the price of finance capital varies widely but in general exceeds the opportunity cost of capital in the economy as a whole, and this leads to the adoption of excessively labour-intensive methods of production, low productivity and low earnings from employment. Here again, a strong case can be made for governments to intervene to improve the structure of incentives.

Market failures also produce adverse unintended effects on the environment. In the market for land, government subsidies often reinforce and exacerbate pressures for the intensive exploitation of natural capital. Part of the problem arises from a neglect by private sector actors of negative externalities associated with production; another part arises from poor management of publicly-owned land and its treatment as a free good; yet another part arises from poorly-defined property rights (whether public or private) governing the use of many natural resources. Governments not only fail to correct the distorted incentive structures which damage the natural stock of capital, they also intensify the problem by subsidising fuel, chemicals and irrigation water used by farmers. These policies place a heavy burden on government budgets and lead countries to follow a comparative advantage based on the intensive use of natural capital rather than human capital. Instead of alleviating the poverty which in some countries is a major cause of environmental degradation, government subsidy programmes enrich upper-income groups and increase inequality in the distribution of income and wealth. One of the important lessons that has emerged from the current discussions on future directions for development is that human development is neither desirable nor possible without sustainable development. There is no inherent conflict between these two seemingly different objectives. In fact, compared to other strategies, a human development strategy relies on an incentive structure which is more compatible with protection and enhancement of the natural environment.

While the costs associated with the exploitation of natural capital have been underestimated, so have the benefits of investing in human capital. A failure to perceive this has led governments, when formulating their trade strategies, to neglect potential long-run comparative advantage based on a skilled, educated labour force able to learn and apply technological innovations. Such a trade strategy requires an active state which takes into account the positive externalities generated by human capital formation and which, by restructuring private incentives or by direct expenditure, compensates for the tendency of the private sector to underinvest in human capital. The appropriate trade strategy is one which promotes an open economy, artificially biased neither towards export promotion nor import substitution. Such a trade regime is the most supportive of human development in the long run.

One must recognise, however, as suggested above, that defects in the incentive system often reflect not market failure but the policies of government itself. We have called special attention to subsidies for water, fertiliser and fuel, although one would want to examine the full range of subsidies when designing a human development strategy for a specific country. It is tempting to characterise policy interventions inimical to human development as examples of government failure, but this would be wrong. The government may simply have pursued different objectives and it would be pointless to accuse it of failing to achieve goals it did not seek.

Where there is genuine government failure, the best remedy may not be to reduce government intervention in the economy, as usually advised, but to correct the failure so that future interventions will do more good than harm. We say this not because we regard government intervention and government expenditure as desirable in themselves but because the very nature of a human development strategy requires an activist state capable of playing a leading role. Human development seldom is served by reducing public expenditure, but it often could be served by altering the composition of public expenditure. The strategy requires not that the government do fewer things but that it do different things. This is the topic of the next chapter.

3 Reallocation of Public Sector Resources

The structure of incentives generates the signals that guide the allocation of resources and influence the division of investment among natural, physical and human capital. The structure of incentives cannot, however, determine the speed of response – the elasticity of supply – to economic opportunities. That depends on other things: initial conditions, institutional arrangements, the capabilities of people and government initiatives. In this chapter we shall focus on the role of government and in particular on the way government expenditure can contribute to human development.

A human development strategy does not necessarily imply that the state will control a larger share of the economy's resources than would occur under a more conventional strategy, but it does imply that the state will use its resources in a fundamentally different way. The strategy is not inherently more costly to the exchequer than conventional strategies, neither in the short nor in the long run. A government that chooses to emphasise human development will have to reallocate its expenditure in favour of human capital activities, but this need not lead to the swollen budgets and enlarged bureaucracies associated with some forms of the welfare state in developed economies. Human development is not a euphemism for the wide array of social policies one typically finds in western Europe; it is a growth and development strategy intended to improve the wellbeing of people in as short a time as possible.

Implementation of the strategy will require a change in the composition of government spending. First, the percentage of the budget earmarked for activities which do not contribute to development should be reduced to a minimum. This includes spending on the military and internal security (which often have little to do with defending the state from external enemies), subsidies for some public enterprises (particularly those – airlines, luxury hotels, breweries – which cater primarily to upper-income groups), excessively large bureaucracies in the public administration (which sometimes have been used to reduce unemployment among the urban educated youth) and external debt service. The revenues thus saved should be used to raise the proportion of expenditure devoted to human development, including greater spending on education and training, basic health and nutrition, fresh water supplies, etc.

Second, within the broad category of human development spending, there should be a reallocation toward those activities which benefit the largest number of people. Spreading resources evenly over large groups rather than concentrating them on small groups is likely to yield a higher rate of return. It will also be more equitable and more consistent with democratic aspirations. In many developing countries this implies giving higher priority to programmes of particular benefit to women and to such things as child nutrition programmes, rural education, small medical clinics and paramedical personnel and to small-scale irrigation projects and other locally based development schemes.

Third, the elaborate, expensive and comprehensive pension and social security systems as found in the West should be avoided, and where they already exist in embryo, their further development should be postponed until they can be extended to the entire population and particularly to those most in need. Most social security schemes in developing countries benefit the urban elite and cannot be justified within a human development strategy. This does not mean, however, that measures to increase economic security must be postponed indefinitely; but it does mean that policies adopted in the developed countries should not be imitated or replicated without careful consideration of costs and benefits and distributive equity. Some feasible programmes for developing countries, oriented towards the poor, are discussed in Chapter 5.

Finally, a human development strategy must walk a fine line between selectivity in public expenditure and the provision of universal services. The conventional wisdom today is that public expenditure should be carefully targeted on selected beneficiaries: leakages to non-beneficiaries should be avoided as much as possible on grounds of economy. In so far as government spending can be accurately targeted on the rural and urban poor, there is something to be said for the conventional wisdom. There are, however, several problems with this approach. First, in many cases relevant to a human development strategy it is not possible to restrict the benefits of public expenditure to specific groups. A farm-to-market road, for example, can be used by anyone in the vicinity, rich and poor alike. A publicly-supported secondary school must be accessible to all children in the community on similar terms; tuition charges for the children of the rich are not really feasible. Second, where selectivity is possible, it often is costly to enforce. Large and elaborate administrative structures may be necessary to exclude undesired beneficiaries or to discriminate positively in favour of intended beneficiaries. The benefits of selectivity may accrue in part to the bureaucrats who administer the programmes, surely not a target group. This is not to deny, for instance, that in some cases user fees for the non-poor and scholarships for the poor are possible, but one should not expect too much of discriminatory charges and subsidies. Third, it may be politically advantageous for tax-supported human development programmes to be universal, open to everyone who wishes to take advantage of them. The gains in terms of national solidarity, full commitment and widespread participation in nationwide development programmes may outweigh the additional costs of organising universal, non-targeted services and projects. This will be especially true if the services are universal in terms of eligibility but are designed to be attractive primarily to certain groups only, so that the intended beneficiaries are largely self-selected. This is a topic to which we return in Chapter 5.

In an empirical study of targeting in nine countries (India, Zambia, Jamaica, Pakistan, Egypt, Sri Lanka, Tunisia, Mexico and the Philippines), Cornia and Stewart examine two common mistakes that occur when targeting public expenditure on specific groups.[1] The first, which they call E-mistakes, occurs when there is excessive coverage of the population, i.e. when persons not intended to be included among the beneficiaries none the less receive benefits. The second, which they call F-mistakes, occurs when persons who were intended to be beneficiaries none the less fail to be covered by the programme and hence fail to receive benefits. Policy often concentrates on minimizing E-mistakes. Yet Cornia and Stewart show that E- and F-mistakes often are inversely related. That is, attempts to reduce the number of E-mistakes often can result in a larger number of F-mistakes.

There are three implications of this analysis for a human development strategy. First, in terms of capabilities and general wellbeing, it should be the purpose of human development as an objective of policy to minimise the number of F-mistakes, to ensure that all those entitled to benefits do in fact receive them. As we discuss in Chapter 4, this does not imply that all programmes should aim for complete coverage, but it does imply that the enhancement of capabilities for all people should be the guiding spirit of public policy. Second, as regards human development as a means, the existence of F-mistakes implies that the future productivity of those persons who failed to be covered by a programme is lower than would otherwise be the case. That is, in so far as human capital expenditure raises the productivity of labour, F-mistakes will entail costs in terms of output forgone. A review of the empirical evidence by Cornia and Stewart suggests that output forgone can be large. Third, all of this suggests that, in designing human development programmes, policymakers should have a bias in favour of broadly-based schemes and not become unduly preoccupied with designing narrowly-targeted schemes.

The reallocation of public expenditure implied by a human development strategy does not entail a trade-off between efficiency and growth. On the contrary, provided an appropriate structure of incentives is put in place, public expenditures in support of human development should increase both allocative efficiency and the rate of growth of personal incomes properly measured. The social rates of return on human development expenditures, when all benefits and costs are taken into account, are quite high. The per capita costs of primary health care and, say, the first twelve years of education are much lower than the costs of university education and urban hospitals. Moreover, the social benefits of investment, when correctly calculated, are usually higher at the base of an expenditure pyramid (e.g. primary education) than at the peak (e.g. doctoral programmes at universities). Thus expenditure on human capital formation can be a very efficient way to promote development.

A healthy, literate, skilled labour force is the foundation of a country's long-term growth. Sharp bursts of growth can be experienced by exploiting natural resources that happen to be in great demand, but unless the economic rents from natural resource extraction are transformed into human capital, such growth is unlikely to be sustainable. The experience of some oil-exporting countries is testimony to this. As the world economy becomes increasingly integrated, the comparative advantage of developing countries, particularly the larger and more populous ones, is likely to rest on the skills, education and technical competence of their labour force. In addition, the existence of a highly-skilled and educated labour force will affect the transfer of technology, making it easier to absorb technical knowledge produced in economically more advanced countries. Similarly, the presence in a developing country of a highly-skilled and educated labour force will make it easier for the country to attract foreign capital. Thus, in numerous ways, a human development strategy is likely to increase the global opportunities open to developing countries. Ultimately, people are a country's principal asset. The benefits of investing in people, however, go beyond the increase in the productivity of labour and access to global opportunities: a healthy, well-educated citizenry contributes to the social cohesion of a country and imparts a dynamism to all aspects of life and culture.

Human development became an attractive policy alternative in reaction to the heavy social costs incurred under orthodox stabilisation and structural adjustment programmes. That is, human development was seen as a way to achieve 'adjustment with a human face'.[2] It can better be understood, however, as a long-term strategy with important implications for short- and medium-term stabilisation programmes.

Adjustment, stabilisation, restructuring – call them what you will, they mean much the same thing – are tactical responses to external shocks and internal macroeconomic disequilibria. These tactical responses should not be allowed to undermine the foundations for long-term development – as occurred in Africa and Latin America during the 'lost decade' of the 1980s – by reducing the rate of human capital formation. If it is necessary in the short term to cut government expenditure, then those items which are of secondary importance should be eliminated and human development expenditures protected. Put another way, human development expenditures constitute the core of a government's development strategy. They are neither luxury items to be added on to conventional development strategies when resources permit, nor are they expendable items that can readily be discarded during periods of retrenchment. They are the heart and soul of government efforts to improve the wellbeing of a nation's people.

A human development strategy, however, like any development strategy, requires political support to sustain it. The reallocation of public expenditure that accompanies the introduction of a human development strategy will create both losers and gainers and, in designing the strategy, the reaction of potential losers should be anticipated. There is an asymmetry during the transition period: those who gained from conventional development strategies and can be expected to lose relatively and perhaps absolutely from a change of strategy are likely to constitute an articulate, well-organised and powerful opposition; the potential beneficiaries, in contrast, while numerically large, are likely to be less articulate, unorganised and politically less influential. Their support for change, moreover, is based merely on an expectation of gain, a gain that bitter experience may have told them is uncertain and possibly long-delayed, whereas the opposition of the minority is based on a virtual certainty of loss, and a loss that will be felt immediately. Thus, while there is potentially a broad base of support for policies of human development, these policies must be carefully selected and crafted to minimise opposition and avoid alienating those in the middle whose net gains or losses will be relatively small.

Political and economic considerations hence point in the same direction: government plans for human development should avoid long lists of desirable but vague objectives which provide little guidance to operational ministries as to how to achieve the objectives. Human development objectives are not moral imperatives. They should be carefully selected on the basis of (i) rigorous technical analysis which weighs benefits and costs, (ii) a political calculation of the number and strength of potential supporters and opponents, and (iii) an assessment of the feasibility and desirability of using some of the benefits to compensate the losers. Whenever a policy change results in a net improvement in the form of a rise in average incomes but is accompanied by a fall in the incomes of some groups, it is in principle possible for the losers to be compensated by the gainers while still leaving the latter better-off. Whether compensation should in fact be paid depends, we suggest, on two things: whether the distribution of income after the policy-change is preferable to the previous distribution and, if so, whether, none the less, the losers must be 'bribed' to acquiesce in the change and not use their political power to frustrate it.

Consider public expenditure on education as an example. It is often said, quite rightly, that human development accords highest priority to primary education, but this generalisation is not a universally established truth and in considering a possible reallocation of public expenditure in favour of primary education, the contributions of secondary and tertiary education should not be overlooked. The social rate of return to different levels of education is something that must be determined, not assumed, and this must be done while taking into account the complementarities that exist among the different levels of education. One example of complementarities is the role of universities in producing well-trained and highly-motivated teachers for primary and secondary education. Apart from the interlinkages among the three tiers of the formal education system, there is a political reason for not neglecting university education; namely, the need to secure the cooperation of the educated classes upon whom much of the success of a human development strategy depends. Moreover, the educated middle classes should be natural allies of human development since the strategy gives high priority to education at all levels, to scientific research and development and to technical change as sources of growth and international competitiveness.

In choosing specific objectives for human development and the sequence of policy initiatives, it is important to take into consideration the degree to which human development programmes can be used to mobilise the participation of the intended beneficiaries. Human development is participatory development and the more people can become directly involved as agents of change, the more successful the overall strategy is likely to be. Campaigns to promote literacy, basic health care, primary education and immunisation of children against epidemic diseases are ideal vehicles for active community participation. Local financial, material and labour resources can be mobilised in support of clearly-defined goals, and local communities can be organised on a permanent basis to monitor progress and ensure that the volume and quality of services are maintained once the campaigns are over.

All of this depends, of course, on selecting goals that are feasible, i.e. capable of being achieved with the resources and administrative capabilities at hand. Excessively ambitious targets should be avoided and careful attention should be paid to the sequence of projects and programmes. One of the distinguishing features of policies that promote human development is that they tend to reinforce one another because of complementarities and positive externalities. As a result, the social benefits of policies frequently exceed by a substantial margin the private benefits, the margin sometimes depending on the order in which projects are undertaken. That is, some policies deserve priority because they facilitate the successful implementation of other policies. Providing access to potable water, for example, is important in its own right and also because it has 'multiplier effects' on such things as the ability to assimilate nutrients from the intake of food, a person's ability to maintain good health and engage in productive activity, and the ability of children to learn. In both the Pakistan and Bangladesh human development reports the education of women was underlined as being critical in attaining a number of other objectives – improved child nutrition, decreased incidence of disease and lower growth of the population.[3] The presumption, in both these illustrations, is, first, that the whole is greater than the sum of its parts and, second, that the sequence in which the parts are assembled affects the benefits of the package as a whole.

All of these considerations make it difficult to quantify the benefits and costs of expenditure on human development. Human capital formation may be analogous to investment in physical capital, but the analogy is far from exact and one must be careful not to apply mechanically the techniques of project appraisal (benefit–cost calculations and the like) that were developed to analyse public sector investments in physical capital to the rather different case of investing in people. None the less, we believe that an effort should be made to estimate benefits and costs so that policymakers can compare expenditure on human development with the returns on other types of expenditure; the alternative is to rely on intuition and guesses. Intuition easily can lead to error, such as underestimating the benefits of human capital formation and hence neglecting expenditure programmes with potentially high returns or, at the other extreme, underestimating the (marginal) costs of human development expenditure and hence expanding expenditure programmes beyond the economically optimum size. These issues are discussed further in Chapter 4.

THE SHAPE OF THE EDUCATION PYRAMID

We turn now to a discussion of the formal education system in developing countries. This sector absorbs more public resources than any other human development activity and the issues raised in allocating tax revenues to education are similar to those that arise in other sectors. Thus it should be possible to apply our analysis to other expenditure programmes with only minor modifications. Formal education, however, is only one way people acquire knowledge. Much knowledge and information are passed on to children, informally, by parents, other relatives and friends. Much is learned through experience, a process at the individual level of learning by doing, of trial and error, experimentation. In some countries skills may be acquired in apprenticeship programmes run by master craftsmen. In others there may be a number of formal training schemes, partially or wholly supported by government. And in still other countries, some of the larger companies may organise their own on-the-job training programmes. Because of the externalities associated with education, and the public goods feature of some forms of education, governments pursuing a human development strategy should always compare the benefits and costs of supporting apprenticeship programmes, public sector training schemes and private sector on-the-job training programmes with the benefits and costs of expenditure on the formal, conventional education system. In what follows below, however, we concentrate on formal education.

In many developing countries budgetary allocations for the formal education system have the shape of an inverted pyramid in which secondary and tertiary education receive more than four times as much public resources as primary education.[4] In many cases primary schools are starved of finance while universities receive heavy subsidies. The majority of the population, particularly the poor, may lack adequate educational facilities, or may find that the opportunity cost of attending school exceeds short-run private benefits, while the children from middle- and upper-class backgrounds benefit from comparatively generously financed university education.[5]

Not only is this inversion of the financial pyramid not equitable, it is also not efficient. Particularly in the poorest developing countries, where primary education has been most neglected,[6] the social rate of return on investing in basic education is high.[7] In addition to high returns, investing in primary education has the advantage of bringing government closer to the people it serves while simultaneously giving people greater control over their own lives and a basic institution of the communities in which they live.

Primary schools are easier for local communities (villages, small towns, urban neighbourhoods) to control than secondary schools, colleges and universities. There is more opportunity for participatory development, for the active involvement of people in education, and hence there is a greater likelihood that educational programmes will enjoy sustained support from the community.

Contrary to common belief, public expenditure on education in developing countries has not in general been an equalising factor, providing equal opportunities to all social classes and groups. There are important exceptions, but more often than not, the educational system is no more egalitarian than the society of which it is a part. The inverted educational expenditure pyramid mirrors the stratification, privilege and discrimination against women and other groups which is characteristic of the society at large. This is hardly surprising, but it suggests that while it might be easy technically to design policies for reallocating resources from tertiary to primary and secondary education, it might be difficult politically to implement such policies. The commitment of the government evidently is crucial, but this in turn depends on securing popular support for human development.

In some circumstances it may be advisable to reallocate expenditure in stages, thereby minimising opposition until a political coalition can be formed to support more wide-ranging measures. In the initial phases of a human development strategy the demand for education by the poor may be low while the middle and upper classes may fully appreciate the advantages of secondary and higher education and press for additional funding. In such circumstances a massive reallocation of resources in favour of basic education should be delayed until the urban and rural poor can be organised to demand a change in priorities.

Even if primary education is free, the opportunity cost to poor families of sending their children to school can be high. In addition to the cost of books and supplies, transport and school uniforms, there is the loss of child labour and resulting decline in household income. At very low levels of income, discount rates may be high and households may be reluctant to give up current income for the sake of a higher income in future. One way of overcoming this problem while adding to human capital formation is to combine an expansion of basic education in poor areas with the introduction of school feeding and child nutrition programmes.

The demand for education by the poor may be depressed for a second reason, namely, a perception that for low-income households the returns to education are low. There is in fact evidence that in both urban and rural areas there are positive connections among additional education, an increase in the productivity of labour and higher incomes.[8] These connections, however, may not be widely understood and it may be necessary as part of a human development strategy to supply the relevant information to the general public.

One aspect of social stratification in developing countries is that not all groups have equal access to formal education, and even in cases where there apparently is equal access, there are enormous variations in the quality of education offered. The rich have greater access than the poor. The urban population has greater access than the rural. There is thus a strong *prima facie* case for reducing the concentration of educational expenditure on high-cost urban colleges and universities and instead distributing resources broadly among the entire population. This implies, in particular, a reallocation of expenditure toward primary and secondary schools, and particularly to schools located in rural areas, where most of the poor are, and where historically education has been severely neglected.

Discriminatory access to education by gender is highly evident throughout the developing world. Women are systematically under-represented at all levels of education. On average in the developing countries the literacy rate of women is only 69 per cent as high as the rate for men. Women receive only 54 per cent as many years of schooling as men. Their enrolment rate in primary school has risen sharply and is now 93 per cent of the men's, but in secondary and tertiary education women lag behind, their enrolment rates being 73 and 53 per cent, respectively, of the men's enrolment rates.[9]

In Pakistan the situation is much worse than the average: three-quarters of the girls have dropped out of primary school before the final year. In the rural areas, among the poorest 20 per cent of the population, over 97 per cent of the women are illiterate, and even among the richest 20 per cent of the rural population, 87 per cent of the women are unable to read and write. The virtual absence of educational opportunities for women in Pakistan is responsible for the poor educational performance of the country as a whole.[10] Although Pakistan is an extreme case, the situation of women in other developing countries such as Bangladesh and Ghana is broadly similar.[11]

Quite apart from educational biases against women, the poor, and rural areas, there is a bias in favour of spending on physical capital and against human capital – teachers, lecturers, instructors, professors. It is sometimes said in the United States that the ideal education consists of Mark Hopkins on one end of a log and a student on the other.[12] The tutorial system at Oxford embodies the same ideal. In many developing countries, however, more emphasis is placed on the log and less on Mark Hopkins. The reason for this is an artificial division of public expenditure between capital and recurrent items, combined with a belief that only capital expenditures contribute to development. The resulting bricks-and-mortar approach to education leads to a misallocation of resources, placing excessive emphasis on school construction (public investment) and insufficient emphasis on teachers and school supplies (spending on which is classified as public consumption). Governments switching to a human development strategy must be careful not to become victims of the way expenditures are classified. Conventional systems of classification make little sense, especially when priority is given to human capital formation.

Returning to the example of Pakistan, its situation suggests that in that country too many resources are devoted to physical capital and as a result insufficient resources are left to produce qualified teachers. Existing school buildings are not used efficiently and the teachers are poorly trained and motivated, unable to provide an education of high quality. Approximately a quarter of all teachers in Pakistan are untrained and the problem is particularly severe in the rural areas where low morale, low pay and few opportunities for advancement have resulted in widespread absenteeism by teachers. Before the students can be educated, something must be done about truancy among the teachers!

One indication of the low efficiency of the educational system in the developing countries as a whole is that in the mid-1980s it took on average nine years of schooling to get one person through grade five. High drop-out rates and high repeat rates represent a waste of resources. It is obvious that in many countries the efficiency of the educational system could be raised by placing less emphasis on building more schools and recruiting more untrained teachers and placing a great deal more emphasis on improving the average quality of primary and secondary education. This implies giving more attention to raising the quality of instruction, lowering the drop-out and repeat rates of students, allocating more money to teaching materials and in general raising the average educational achievements of the stock of human capital represented by students. In other words, in many cases the human and physical resources already allocated to education can be used more intensively and more efficiently.

Developing countries potentially have a comparative advantage in education because teaching is a labour-intensive activity and labour is relatively abundant in developing countries. Of course, education requires skilled labour and that is often in short supply, but this is a reason for altering the allocation of investment to enable developing countries to exploit their potential comparative advantage, not a reason for perpetuating the *status quo*. That is, compared to other 'industries', education uses a factor of production (educated labour) that potentially is rather cheap in developing countries, particularly in countries committed to a human development strategy. Thus education often is and certainly could be a low-cost industry in developing countries. This is reflected in the rate of return on educational investment. Actual and potential future returns on expenditure on education are attractive in part because the benefits are high and in part because the costs are low.

Despite this, there has been underinvestment in education. In 1985, for instance, public expenditure on education was only $27 per inhabitant in the developing countries as compared to $515 in the developed countries, a ratio of 1:19. That is, relative to income, the developing countries spend far less on education than the developed countries. Within the education budget, the developing countries spend proportionately much less on teaching materials. In Japan, for example, 6.5 per cent of the education budget is allocated to teaching materials; in India, only 1.3 per cent. Finally, within the education budget, and relative to the distribution of students across primary, secondary and tertiary education, the developing countries spend proportionately much less than the developed countries on the first two tiers of the pyramid. In Japan, for example, 38.2 per cent of the education budget is allocated to primary education, where 50 per cent of the students are enrolled. Thus the expenditure/enrolment ratio is 0.8. The ratios in secondary and tertiary education in Japan are 0.9 and 1.1, respectively. In Nigeria, in contrast, the expenditure/enrolment ratio is 0.2 at the primary level, 2.0 at the secondary level and 21.7 at the tertiary level.[13] There is thus tremendous scope for improving the average quality of education in developing countries even within the existing inadequate budgetary allocations.

In the short term, the most cost-effective way of improving primary education may be to use existing facilities more intensively and provide additional training for existing teachers. Quality could be improved and student drop-out rates reduced if teachers were to become accountable to the communities they serve, and not solely to ministries of education in distant capital cities. A human development strategy should attempt to transform local primary and secondary schools into centres of community action, with parents and other members of the locality taking an active role in educational and other activities concerned with human development, such as literacy campaigns, the construction and maintenance of health clinics, the construction of sanitation facilities and the provision of potable water supplies.

There are also financial benefits of actively involving members of the community in local education. Under appropriate circumstances parents, friends and neighbours can help to reduce the costs to the exchequer of primary education – for example, by donating their labour and local materials for construction and school maintenance activities. The essential objective is to mobilise local talents, skills and energy to accelerate human capital formation in the locality for the benefit of everyone, children and adults alike. This will not happen spontaneously but will require the creation of an institutional mechanism which fosters cooperation between teachers and the rest of the community, which motivates and rewards good teachers and gives them stature in the community, and which encourages widespread participation by the community in educational and other development activities. Only in this way is it possible to ensure that investments in education meet the genuine needs of the people.

Even if more resources cannot be allocated to the education sector as a whole, the allocation of additional resources to primary education at the expense of the other two tiers of the pyramid need not inflict serious harm on secondary and university education. Costs per student-year in primary education typically are only a fraction of the cost per student-year in secondary and university education and consequently a marginal redistribution from the upper tiers to the lower could make a more than marginal improvement in primary education possible. This would be particularly true if, at the same time, repeat rates in primary education could be reduced. In Brazil, for example, the 'unit cost' in tertiary education was 7.5 times that in primary education in 1985. Thus, if the number of student-years at university were reduced by 100 it would be possible to provide, at the same cost, 750 additional student-years of primary education. If at the same time the primary school repeat rate in Brazil could be reduced from 20 per cent (in 1988) to, say, 2 per cent (the rate in the Philippines) an additional 135 children could be given a primary education. Thus the opportunity cost of 100 university places in this example is 885 primary school places.

It should be clear from the above illustration that the diversion of even modest sums from universities and colleges can have magnified effects on primary education. Moreover, since the beneficiaries of higher education often come from families able to pay for all or part of their education, it may be possible to recover some of the costs of tertiary education by imposing (or raising) tuition fees. In this way public expenditure on primary and secondary education could be increased without a corresponding reduction in public and private revenues available for university education. There is hence a strong case to be made for introducing an equitable system of fees and loans to replace the heavy subsidies now received by higher education.

The level of expenditure that can be justified for each of the three tiers of the education pyramid depends in part on considerations of equity and in part on the social rates of return on expenditure at each tier. The latter in turn depend on the balance of supply and demand for different types of human capital, a balance that will vary with the level of development. Every developing country obviously needs trained scientists, engineers, managers and teachers – and other people with professional and technical skills. The issue, thus, is not whether resources should be devoted to tertiary education, but how large an allocation of limited public revenues tertiary education should receive.

Many highly-educated people in developing countries lack opportunities to apply their skills and talents. This suggests a relative excess of supply and an inefficient use of the existing stock of human capital. Poor utilisation of highly-educated people lowers both the private and social rates of return on expenditure on tertiary education, compared to the return to primary and secondary education. Many educated people either become unemployed or emigrate to developed countries. This 'human capital flight' or 'brain drain' constitutes a loss of resources to developing countries and a poor investment of public funds. The correct response to this problem is to change the composition of public expenditure toward areas where returns are higher while also introducing measures to ensure that all available human capital is productively employed. Policies which lead to an open economy can be particularly helpful. Countries which exploit dynamic comparative advantages based on the skill, technical sophistication and education of its workers will be well-placed to create remunerative employment for its university graduates and other highly-skilled people.

ACCESS OF ALL TO PRIMARY HEALTH CARE

As with education, so too in health: there is an inverted expenditure pyramid in most developing countries. About three-quarters of all public expenditure on health is for expensive medical care that benefits a small minority of the population living in the urban areas. A high proportion of the budget for health, 80 to 90 per cent in some countries, is spent on hospitals, almost all of which are located in the cities. At the same time, only about 60 per cent of the people have access to primary health care. A high proportion of the poor, and of those living in rural areas, are not reached by the health care system and are forced to rely on home remedies and traditional medicine.

It is impossible to justify the pattern of expenditure one encounters in most developing countries. Viewed from the perspective of human development, the budgetary allocations are both inefficient and inequitable, and a major change in priorities clearly is desirable.[14] What are needed are a switch from hospitals to primary health care and a change of emphasis from curative to preventive medicine. Such a change in health strategy should make it possible to provide access for all to basic health at a cost the country can readily afford.

Indeed, by emphasising primary health care it often will be possible to improve the average health of the population quite considerably while simultaneously reducing total expenditure on health programmes. It is possible to get more health for less money precisely because existing resources are used so blatantly inefficiently. There are a number of inexpensive preventive health programmes which, if implemented on a nationwide basis, can reduce the need for more expensive curative health care. Examples include mass immunisation against communicable diseases, pre-natal care combined with post-natal maternity and child care programmes, and sanitation programmes designed to eliminate water-borne diseases. Introduction of such relatively simple public health measures could lead to a sharp reduction in the need for hospitals, doctors and medical technicians, expensive equipment and medicines and consequently to large savings of government revenue.

Beyond the immediate, direct effects of an expanded public health programme, there are longer-term benefits in the form of fewer days lost from work because of illness, a higher productivity of labour and increased household incomes, a part of which can be saved and invested in growth-promoting activities. The adverse consequences of poor health are sometimes irreversible, persisting over an entire lifetime and beyond. Unlike most educational deficiencies, which often can be corrected later, serious health problems early in life sometimes cannot be corrected in later years and their negative effects on productivity, incomes and general wellbeing can last indefinitely. Indeed, the effects of disease and malnutrition can be passed from one generation to the next. For example, the low birth-weight and poor nutrition of an infant girl can cause her later as a mother to bear children with low birth-weight or poorly-developed mental capacities. The costs of preventing such things are low and represent an investment in human capital with a high pay-off. Not to spend the money would be inhumane.

Thus the argument for reallocating public expenditure from costly curative care (hospitals and doctors) to inexpensive preventive care (local health clinics staffed by paramedical personnel) is powerful. Indeed, because an expansion of preventive health measures reduces the need for expenditure on curative health measures, the case for a reallocation of resources in favour of primary health care may be even stronger than the case for reallocating resources in favour of primary and secondary education.

One must not push this reasoning too far, however. The design of human development strategies puts a premium on lateral thinking, on breaking down old categories and on seeing connections that previously had been overlooked. The strong complementarities between expenditures on health and education are a case in point. Students who enjoy good health, for example, also benefit from an increased ability to learn. At the same time, people who enjoy a good education also are likely to know how best to maintain good health. Causality thus runs in both directions. Hence a reallocation of public expenditure to both primary health care and primary education can have a beneficial impact on each area of activity which is mutually reinforcing. Once again, the whole is likely to be greater than the sum of its parts.

There are considerable advantages therefore in concentrating on primary health care and the two lower tiers of the education pyramid in the early stages of a human development strategy. Spending on preventive health measures is particularly attractive because it represents a low-cost way of combating many of the most common diseases found in developing countries. In Bangladesh, for instance, half of all deaths are among children under five years of age and two-thirds of these deaths, namely those caused by diarrhoea, measles and tetanus, could be prevented at negligible cost, by immunisation or simple treatments. In fact a recent child-immunisation campaign in Bangladesh was remarkably successful and about 70 per cent of all infants were reached. The cost of this programme, which surely will save a great many lives, was only 0.3 per cent of total public revenue.

The basic components of a primary health care system are few in number, simple to implement and inexpensive. The six key elements are (i) immunisation against the six most common communicable diseases, namely, measles, diphtheria, whooping cough, polio, tuberculosis and tetanus, (ii) nationwide availability of about 15 to 20 essential generic drugs, (iii) widespread availability and use of oral rehydration therapy, (iv) a family planning, midwifery and pregnancy management programme, (v) improved water supply and sanitation and (vi) health education. The immunisation programme costs only about $1.20 per child; the per capita cost of the generic drugs programme is about half that amount; and a dose of the simple mixture used in oral rehydration costs only $0.10. Given the low costs and high effectiveness of these first three elements of a basic health programme, they obviously should be given very high priority in a human development strategy. Implementation does not require hospitals and large numbers of doctors; paramedical personnel will suffice; and diffusion can occur through mass grassroots campaigns.

To be fully successful, however, these initiatives should form part of a wider set of interventions which include the provision of clean water supplies, improved sanitation and infant nutrition programmes. Also important are family-planning programmes which, by providing information, education and contraceptive supplies, can considerably improve the wellbeing of families, and particularly women, by enabling them to choose the number of children they bring into the world. None of these need be expensive when compared to conventional health expenditure programmes in developing countries and the ratio of benefits to costs will be a great deal higher.

Clean water is essential for improved public health. Diarrhoeal disease, the single most important cause of infant and child deaths, cannot effectively be combatted without it. Moreover, inexpensive, technologically appropriate methods for supplying potable water to the urban and rural poor exist and can readily be introduced: public tube wells, rainwater collectors, gravity-fed water distribution systems and hand-pumps. Hand-pumps are a particularly attractive solution because they are low in cost while being simple to install, use and maintain. None of these technologies, however, is expensive and it has been estimated in Asia that it should be possible to provide potable water to everyone at an annual cost of about $2.00 per person.

Basic sanitation also is essential for good health. Particularly in the humid tropics where average temperature and humidity levels are high, and high population densities bring people into close proximity, disease is easily spread. Yet, in many countries in the humid tropics, basic sanitation is woefully inadequate. In Bangladesh, for example, only about 10 per cent of the population have sanitary ways to dispose of human excreta. There has been a small government programme since the 1950s to supply subsidised pit latrines, but even after four decades only about 6 per cent of households have them. Given the appalling sanitary conditions and the lack of success of past policies, the country clearly needs a 'sanitation revolution' as recommended in a recent human development report.[15] Rather than rely on subsidised latrines supplied by the central government, it is recommended that the new approach centre on the active involvement of local communities, including non-governmental organisations and private enterprise.

The details of the technology and the delivery system will, of course, vary from one country to another. What is important to notice is that in the two cases of potable water and adequate sanitation, improvements in health are not directly related to increased public spending on conventional health programmes. In these two cases, indeed, the average health of the population would rise if fewer resources were allocated to the ministry of health (for spending on hospitals, etc.) and more were allocated, say, to ministries concerned with water supply and drainage.

A similar situation arises in the case of nutrition. Malnutrition is a major cause of poor health in developing countries and even in the United States 25 million people threatened by hunger receive 'food stamps' under a national anti-poverty programme. In developing countries, as in developed ones, hunger and malnutrition have relatively little to do with the aggregate supply of food but instead reflect the way society is organised and particularly the distribution of wealth and income that flow from that organisation.[16] People are hungry either because they lack the productive resources – land, other fixed assets, water – to grow enough food for themselves or the money to buy it. The fundamental solution to the problem of malnutrition thus has much more to do with creating productive employment and achieving a more even distribution of income and wealth than with increasing public expenditure on health. None the less, short of the structural reforms discussed in Chapter 4, the problem can at least be ameliorated by school feeding programmes and food subsidies directed to lactating mothers and infants.

The experience of Thailand is instructive.[17] In 1981 about 51 per cent of the country's pre-school children suffered from protein-energy malnutrition. The following year a series of reforms were introduced which changed priorities in favour of (i) preventive health measures, (ii) primary health care, with an emphasis on nutrition, clean water and sanitation, essential drugs and immunisation, and (iii) community involvement in administration, financing and decision-taking through village committees and village health communicators and volunteers. The results were spectacular. By 1989, protein-energy malnutrition had fallen to 21 per cent, the infant mortality rate had declined from 41 per 1000 in 1981 to 28 per 1000, access of households to clean water had risen from 32 per cent in 1982 to 78 per cent and 98 per cent of all villages were participating in the primary health care programme.

A human development strategy entails the construction of a basic health care system accessible to all and this, in turn, implies a reallocation of public expenditure away from expensive curative equipment, urban hospitals, the training of large numbers of doctors and the payment of their high salaries once they start to practise conventional medicine. Thailand shows it can be done. This will happen, however, only if the government is strongly committed to the strategy and understands that both the social rate of return and equity would be improved by a reorientation of policy. After all, expensive, curative-oriented and inequitable health systems exist in developing countries because the political and economic elites demand it. What is needed is a countervailing demand from the beneficiaries of a human development strategy for a low-cost, prevention-oriented and more equitable public health system.

This does not imply that there is no role for private medicine in developing countries, but the thrust of the health care system must be preventive measures organised by the state. The private sector can then fill in the gaps and supply the more elaborate and expensive treatments to those who can afford them. At present, the poor spend proportionately more of their income on health services than the rich, while suffering much worse health. In Bangladesh, for instance, the poorest families spend about 5 per cent of their income on private health whereas the richest families spend only about 1.8 per cent. This occurs despite the fact that public health facilities are virtually free in Bangladesh. The reasons are that most people do not have access to public facilities because the facilities are located in the cities and, moreover, those who do have access receive a low quality of care. As a result only one patient in four seeks treatment from them. That is, the government is spending its health-care money on the wrong things, and doing them badly.

A government committed to human development obviously has to construct facilities in the rural regions of the country. Equally important, it must ensure that these facilities are adequately staffed with properly-trained paramedical personnel, that a few basic medicines and other supplies are available and that there is an active outreach programme to inform the people of what is on offer and how the services can best be used.

As with expenditures on formal education, governments commonly regard construction of facilities as capital expenditure (and hence contributing to development) and spending on staff, medical supplies and health education as recurrent expenditure (and hence not contributing to development). While it would be wrong to reverse the assumptions, some recurrent expenditure should be regarded as contributing to human capital formation. In Pakistan, however, about three-quarters of recurrent health expenditure is allocated to hospitals and medical training – despite the fact that the country has an excess supply of doctors (at prevailing salaries) and many secondary hospitals have low occupancy rates. This pattern of spending is neither equitable nor efficient.

A significant proportion of recurrent costs could be recovered by imposing discriminatory user fees and the funds thereby released could be channelled to primary health clinics for the benefit of, say, mothers and children, or the residents of rural areas or the poor in general. There should be little difficulty in principle in designing a structure of user fees so that they are progressive, with only a modest burden falling on the poor.[18] The easiest way to do this is not to devise a structure of charges based on the ability of specific users to pay but, instead, to levy uniform charges on those services largely consumed by upper-income groups. For example, in countries such as Pakistan, where there has been a relative overinvestment in producing doctors, students wishing to acquire a medical education should be required to bear the full cost, perhaps assisted by a government-funded loan. Similarly, charges for medical services at teaching hospitals could be higher than elsewhere, since such hospitals cater disproportionately to upper-income urban residents. Lower charges would occur at secondary hospitals and services at basic health clinics could be free.

The structure of fees would thus provide a strong incentive to people to use the health clinics rather than hospitals. Pecuniary incentives will not suffice, however; community involvement in basic health programmes also is critical to success. Bangladesh, for example, is self-sufficient in oral rehydration salts, but oral rehydration methods are used in only 15 to 20 per cent of the relevant cases. The problem in this instance is not supply but effective demand. People need to become educated in basic health issues and to become actively involved in primary health care. Grassroots organisations and local government, not central government, are likely to be most effective in ensuring that basic services actually reach those most in need. In the area of health care, as in many other areas of human development, a strategy based on development by the people, not just for the people, is likely to be most successful in attaining its objectives.

REDUCING LOW-PRIORITY PUBLIC EXPENDITURE

A human development strategy naturally tends to call attention to the potential benefits of reallocating public resources in favour of human capital, such as basic health services and primary education. Within the education and health budgets both equity and efficiency often can be increased by shifting priorities from services at the top of the pyramid (which usually favour upper-income groups disproportionately) to those at the bottom (which favour lower-income groups). These intersectoral and intrasectoral reallocations pose the question of what areas of public expenditure should bear the burden of substantial reductions. This question cannot, of course, be answered in the abstract since the details of government spending will vary from one country to another, but areas worth investigating include debt servicing, military expenditure, internal security and subsidies to the rich. In some countries it may also be possible to reduce public spending on state enterprises either by privatising some of them or reducing their deficits, or by a combination of the two.

(i) Debt Servicing

The external debt of developing countries more than doubled between 1980 and 1990. By 1989 repayment of interest and capital on the debt was $171 billion, of which interest alone was more than $64 billion, and the total would have been larger still, had not many countries fallen into arrears. Because of these heavy debt service payments, during the second half of the 1980s there was a net transfer of resources from poor countries to rich of almost $200 billion, resources which in principle could have been used to promote human development.

In a number of countries, particularly in sub-Saharan Africa and Latin America, debt servicing has become a major item of government expenditure. Indeed, debt repayment often is even greater than military expenditure. More important, the burden of servicing the external debt has fallen disproportionately on the poor, the working class in general and on sections of the middle class. In order to make resources available for debt servicing, governments have been forced to reduce their deficits and they have often done this by cutting expenditures on human development. As a result, the role of the state in actively promoting development has been curtailed. Overwhelmed by external debt and unable to raise taxes sufficiently, many governments have increased their domestic indebtedness to the banking system or resorted to inflationary finance through the central bank.

In order to amass the foreign exchange necessary to service the external debt, many countries have felt compelled to adopt a 'neo-mercantilist' policy, maximising exports and minimising imports by restricting aggregate demand, imposing import restrictions and devaluing the exchange rate; in addition, some export incentives have been introduced. Since the neo-mercantilist policies have coincided with a period of recession in the developed countries (including the ex-socialist developed countries), the effect has been to worsen the commodity terms of trade of the developing countries, thereby aggravating their economic hardship. The developed countries, in turn, have responded by increasing their own protectionist barriers, thereby reducing the rate of growth of world trade.

Perhaps even more serious in the long run, some developing countries have used contractionary monetary and fiscal policies to lower real wage rates in an attempt to become more competitive in international markets. Competitiveness based on compressed real wages, however, is at best short-lived. In the long-term it weakens an economy's ability to shift resources into activities where higher productivity and higher incomes are possible. What is needed instead is an activist state committed to human development which gives highest priority to ensuring that the labour force is literate, skilled and well-educated.

One reason why the governments of developing countries became so deeply embroiled in disputes over debt repayments is that they unwisely agreed to guarantee (and in some cases take over entirely) foreign loans extended to private domestic corporations and banks. A situation of 'moral hazard' was created whereby neither the overseas lender nor the local borrower had an incentive to act prudently. By guaranteeing the liabilities of private enterprises, the governments of developing countries in effect granted enormous subsidies to the private sector and, when the liabilities became payable, the general public was expected to foot the bill. When the debt crisis erupted in Mexico in 1982, for example, the government nationalised the private banks, in part to relieve them of their debt-repayment difficulties. Something similar occurred in Chile a year later.[19] These problems were not limited to the private sector, however: in many countries the government also guaranteed the foreign debts of public and semi-public corporations.

In some cases external borrowing led directly to capital flight. That is, external debts were incurred in order to finance the accumulation of external assets by wealthy private citizens. In the Philippines, for instance, a revolving door seems to have operated: foreign loans were obtained in order to acquire foreign assets; these foreign assets were then used as collateral for more foreign loans to acquire more foreign assets. It has been estimated that in the Philippines capital flight was equivalent to about 70 per cent of the foreign debt, and the proportions are thought to be even higher in Argentina, Venezuela and Mexico.[20]

The most seriously indebted developing countries would have to experience unprecedentedly rapid growth in the 1990s just to recover the ground lost in the 1980s and place themselves in a position to resume the rate of

growth enjoyed in the fifteen years after 1965. The basis for sustained
accelerated growth, however, is lacking because investment in human and
physical capital was neglected during the years of economic crisis. The
much-discussed structural adjustment policies, far from laying the foundation for future growth as their advocates claim, have actually weakened
development prospects.[21]

Given the situation facing the most heavily-indebted countries, particularly the very low-income economies in sub-Saharan Africa, the prospects
for human development almost certainly will be meagre unless some relief
is forthcoming. Three broad possibilities are conceivable. First, there could
be a very substantial increase in foreign aid in the form of grants, so that the
negative resource transfer becomes positive and large enough to permit
adequate funding of a human development strategy. Alternatively, second,
the foreign debt could be cancelled, in whole or in large part, and the loan
in effect converted into a grant. Failing the above two remedies, some
developing countries may have no alternative but to default. This is clearly
a measure of last resort, although one with many historical precedents, and
if forced to choose between paying foreign creditors and preventing further
suffering of their own people, some governments may take debt relief into
their own hands. This would be a pity, since the cost of solving the foreign
debt problem of sub-Saharan Africa and many of the other heavily indebted
countries is relatively modest.

(ii) Expenditure on the Military and Internal Security

In many developing countries, expenditure on the military and internal
security represent a massive diversion of public resources to socially waste-
ful purposes. Considering just military expenditure, and ignoring expenditure on internal security, there appears to be a rough inverse association
between the level of human development and the percentage of total income
absorbed by the military. For example, in 1989 the developing countries
classified by UNDP as 'high human development' allocated 3.1 per cent of
their gross domestic product to military expenditure. The 'medium human
development' countries excluding China allocated 4.5 per cent and the 'low
human development' countries excluding India allocated 4.8 per cent. There
is thus a *prima facie* case for enquiring, in every country contemplating
adopting a human development strategy, whether it would be possible to
reduce the resources allocated to the army, navy, air force, intelligence
services and secret police, paramilitary units, local police, etc., in order to
increase outlays on more productive activities.

Military expenditure and debt servicing account for a high proportion of total expenditure in many developing countries and the two items often are closely connected. In fact more than a third of the total external debt of developing countries was incurred to acquire military equipment. Moreover, recent research suggests that the availability of external loans actually increases the propensity of governments to spend on the military.[22] Foreign aid, in this case, makes no contribution to development, unless of course military expenditure is thought, rather implausibly, to contribute indirectly to human development. It is not uncommon for military expenditure and payments on the foreign debt to absorb 40–80 per cent of current government revenue. For example, in 1987 these two items accounted for 55 per cent of government revenue in Sri Lanka, 61 per cent in Pakistan, 64 per cent in the Philippines, 65 per cent in Colombia and 85 per cent in Jordan.[23]

Between 1960 and 1988 military spending in developing countries increased fivefold in constant US dollars and grew twice as fast as income per head.[24] In the late 1980s the rate of growth of spending on the military declined somewhat, but it could well increase again in the 1990s. Conflicts within states rather than conflicts between states are likely to increase as sub-nationalist movements challenge the legitimacy not only of specific governments but of the state itself. Indeed in 1988, of the 111 conflicts in the developing world, 90 per cent were intra-state struggles.[25]

Rivalry between the two superpowers once provided the stimulus to militarisation in developing countries, but since the collapse of the Soviet Union, a new impulse has become important, namely the quest of arms manufacturers to seek out new or expanded markets in developing countries to compensate for the loss of markets in the developed countries. There is a danger that the end of the Cold War will foreshadow not an era of global peace but an explosion of sub-nationalist conflicts throughout the world. In the final years of the Cold War imports of military equipment and supplies accounted for seven per cent of total imports in developing countries[26] and between 1978 and 1988 developing countries accounted for more than three-quarters of all arms traded internationally.[27] The risk today is that these percentages will increase.

Military expenditure already is a major obstacle to human development. Indeed military spending in developing countries is greater than spending on education and health combined. Despite an evident decline in external threats to national security, many governments continue to spend large sums on the armed forces and on internal security. Providing security to its citizens is one of the first responsibilities of a government and a lack of internal security can be a severe brake on development. Spending on inter-

· nal security, however, is often intended not to enhance the security of the citizenry but to protect the government or the state from its own people, or to enable small minorities to suppress the majority and retain political power. In many countries spending on the armed forces serves no purpose other than keeping the armed forces in power at the expense (financially and politically) of the civilian population. The experience of Costa Rica, which has managed to do without a military establishment, is enlightening.

Accurate information on the amount of resources allocated to internal security is difficult to obtain. In countries racked by ethnic and religious conflicts – Sri Lanka, Ethiopia, India, Somalia, Angola – expenditures on internal policing and suppressing rebellion are substantial, often greater than central government expenditure on human development activities. Some of this is inescapable, and the difficulties of containing domestic conflict in pluralist states should not be minimised, but much domestic violence could be avoided by encouraging democratic political participation by all groups and, where the aspirations of sub-nationalist movements prove to be irreconcilable, by peacefully acceding to secessionist demands. The non-violent separation of Czechoslovakia into two states shows how it should be done.

Democracy and internal security often go hand-in-hand. That is, in many countries it will not be possible to reduce expenditure on internal security unless democratic practices are introduced throughout the political life of the country. This is recognised in the human development report on Colombia, where a distinction is made between 'negotiable' and 'non-negotiable' violence.[28]

Since the eruption of *la violencia* in 1948 after the assassination of a political leader of the populist left, Colombia has attempted, unsuccessfully, to cope with widespread social violence by suppression. Recently, however, there has been a change of approach and 'negotiable' violence has been reduced by extending a political amnesty to members of the various guerrilla movements and integrating the ex-combatants into the electoral process. So far at least, greater democracy in Colombia appears to have succeeded in reducing political violence. On the other hand, 'non-negotiable' violence, i.e. violence that has its roots in such structural problems as poverty, unemployment and lack of human development, persists. Here the solution is neither suppression (internal security) nor democratisation but a frontal assault on the structural causes.

In the case of non-negotiable violence, human development may be necessary to permit a reduction in expenditure on internal security. We thus have a possible virtuous circle: expenditure on human development weakens the structural causes of non-negotiable violence; this leads to reduced social conflict, which in turn allows a reduction in spending on internal security; less spending on internal security releases resources for human development, which further weakens the structural causes of non-negotiable violence. In the course of this virtuous circle the role and influence of the military and security forces can be progressively reduced as their *raison d'être* diminishes.

(iii) Public Sector Enterprises

In many developing countries the losses of public sector enterprises constitute a substantial drain on central government revenues and it is natural to consider whether the drain can be reduced and the resources thereby released used for other purposes. The sale of state enterprises to either domestic or foreign buyers is one possible option – and a rather fashionable one at present – but this is not the only option and the full range of possibilities should be considered before embarking on a particular course of action.

State enterprises in developing countries have a long history. They first became a conscious instrument of development in Turkey, spread to Latin America (Mexico, Brazil, Chile) in the 1930s and then became the dominant form of property ownership in the socialist countries (China, Cuba, Vietnam). The role they have played has varied enormously and it would be quite wrong to assume that whenever state enterprises operate at a loss, human development would best be served by disposal of these assets. Whenever a sale is contemplated, one should first ask three questions. (i) Is it desirable to subsidise the enterprise and, if so, why? (ii) Which groups in society benefit from the subsidy? (iii) If a subsidy is desirable neither on grounds of economic efficiency nor of equity, would it be possible to eliminate the subsidy by lowering costs or raising revenues and, if so, would this be better than an outright sale?

The answers to these questions should be determined on a case-by-case basis. For example, a subsidy may be justified on efficiency grounds where there is a market failure. If a state enterprise organises training programmes that benefit other employers too or a research programme which produces knowledge which is not entirely firm-specific, benefits are produced for society as a whole which are not fully captured by the firm's revenue stream. In such cases a subsidy to cover the gap between social and private benefits would be appropriate. Note, however, that market failure can be used to justify a fixed level of subsidy only, not losses of indefinite magnitude.

Similarly, even if there is no market failure, a subsidy may be justified on income distribution grounds. Often, however, subsidies are in fact used to cover the losses of state enterprises that provide services mainly consumed by the middle- and upper-income groups. Examples include urban telephone services, luxury hotels and national airlines. Clearly, improvements in the distribution of income cannot be used as valid reasons for subsidies in cases such as these. Moreover, even if the subsidies do benefit largely the poor, and hence diminished inequality can reasonably be adduced, one must still consider whether the distributional objectives could not be achieved at lower cost by some other means. Only if it is impossible for political or technical reasons to redistribute income through the tax and transfer systems would it be sensible to use the deficits of state enterprises to redistribute income to the poor.

Assuming that continued subsidy by the state cannot be justified, policymakers must decide whether to transfer state enterprises to the private sector or to reform the state enterprises while keeping them in the public sector. The possibility of reform should not be ruled out. If the losses are due to government-imposed prices below a market clearing level, it might be possible to eliminate the subsidies by allowing state enterprises to set their own prices. If the losses are due to unnecessarily high costs, such as those caused by over-manning, then a possible solution is to terminate the subsidies and encourage state firms to cut their costs. It would be arbitrary to assume that under no circumstances are state enterprises able to cover their costs and earn a profit for their owners, the taxpayers.

Ultimately the decision between private and public ownership should depend on the social rate of return. If the assets will earn a higher social rate of return in the private sector, they should be sold; if not, they should be kept in the public sector. In practice, a human development strategy is likely to entail some transfer of state enterprises to the private sector, namely, those loss-making enterprises which cater primarily to the rich. At the same time there could well be an expansion of public sector enterprises providing services that are essential for human development but that cannot be supplied efficiently by the private sector.[29] Examples include the supply of electric power to rural areas, an underground urban transport system, urban water and sewage. Thus a human development strategy would not necessarily lead to a smaller state enterprise sector, but it probably would lead to a different composition of the state enterprise sector.

The question thus is not whether the state should own some enterprises, but which enterprises would contribute most to development by becoming or remaining part of the public sector. In some countries, alas, unless the management of the public sector is overhauled, the answer to the question might be 'none'. In many developing countries public enterprises are plagued by serious problems which undermine their efficiency and lead to large losses. These losses in turn create serious difficulties for the central bank and the ministry of finance. The government feels compelled to provide financial support for the state enterprises, yet often requires little financial discipline of them. State enterprises face what is sometimes called a soft budget constraint.[30] Unlike private firms, state enterprises are not allowed to go bankrupt, nor are they subject to the threat of a hostile corporate take-over, nor are they required to raise capital by borrowing on the private capital market. They thus avoid outside scrutiny of their economic perform-ance. At the same time, politicians often interfere in their operations. Since many state enterprises are monopolies, they are not forced by competition to respond to consumer demands or to hold down labour costs. In extreme cases they can become breeding grounds for corruption – by politicians, managers and workers.

A human development strategy should regard these problems not as immutable facts of life but as issues requiring attention. Many state enter-prises could become financially viable and even transformed into a source of revenue for government simply by being forced to become more com-mercially-oriented. The government could, for example, remove their subsi-dies, end their concessional loans, require state enterprises to pay the same taxes as private enterprises and in return give the managers of state enter-prises more freedom as regards pricing and investment policies. Reforms of this type are a feasible alternative to privatisation.[31]

Many public enterprises were created originally because of market fail-ures of one sort or another: because they supplied public goods, because of external social benefits, because economies of scale gave rise to natural monopolies, because private enterprise was weak and undeveloped and could not raise equity capital. Where these market failures persist, privati-sation is unlikely to be a success. But as countries develop and grow, markets are likely to function more efficiently and private enterprise will be able to play a larger role in the newly-emerging sectors of the economy. Moreover, as the economy grows the private capital market is increasingly likely to be able to mobilise the financial resources needed to purchase public enterprises from the government. The private capital market should also find it easier to finance new projects. Exceptionally large projects, however, may continue to exceed the funding capabilities of the capital market and if so, state-owned development banks may be able to fill the gaps in the capital market while continuing to provide resources to those activities, such as physical infrastructure, which are socially beneficial but unattractive to private investors.

State enterprises, in other words, are likely to be part of a human development strategy. Wholesale privatisation is unlikely to be desirable, although it may be sensible for some state enterprises to be sold to the private sector. The essential point is that the state enterprises should not be allowed to operate at a loss, unless losses can be fully justified by market failures, or there are desirable changes in the distribution of income that cannot be achieved more efficiently by other means. Every effort must be made to prevent losses by state enterprises from absorbing public revenues that could better be spent on human development. In many cases it should be possible to reform the state enterprise sector, eliminate the drain on public expenditure and increase the volume of resources available for supporting human capital formation. Only where reform is impossible, or where the private sector clearly is able to obtain a higher social rate of return, should state enterprises systematically be closed down or sold. Elsewhere, under appropriate conditions, the state enterprises should be expected to make a profit, part of which should be turned over to the government to enhance its income and increase the financial resources available for human development.

(iv) Subsidies to the Rich

One of the themes running through our analysis of public expenditure is that a disproportionate share of the benefits has been captured by upper-income groups. These groups may or may not be the explicit targets of subsidies, but the fact remains that they are often the major beneficiaries. This is true whether one is concerned with health expenditure, education, housing subsidies, the deficits of state enterprises or, as we shall see, the pricing of urban utilities or government subsidies of productive inputs used in agriculture.

Government investments in a broad range of urban amenities – water, electricity, gas and sewage – often do relatively little to improve the well-being of the poor.[32] In cities such as Lima, Peru the middle and upper classes have clean water piped to their homes and pay water charges which fail to cover capital and running costs, i.e. they are subsidised. The poor living in the barrios, in contrast, have no piped water supply but instead obtain water from private contractors who haul it in by truck and of course sell it at a price which covers all their costs and produces a profit. Costa Rica, generally speaking, is an exception. It has an impressive record of human development and has skilfully used some public subsidies to benefit its poorer citizens. Even in Costa Rica, however, many of the subsidies provide more help to the rich than to the poor. In education, for example, data for 1983 indicate that two-thirds of the subsidies were to the urban areas and fully a third was used to subsidise higher education. The poor received few of these benefits. The same is true of subsidies for housing, water supply and sanitation. Housing subsidies were used to reduce the interest rates paid on home loans. Ninety per cent of the subsidised loans went to urban families. The 26 per cent of the people who were poor received only 11 per cent of the housing subsidies and 20 per cent of the subsidies for water and sanitation. The 12 per cent of those living in extreme poverty received none of the housing subsidies and only 9 per cent of water and sanitation subsidies.[33] A case has been made in Colombia for eliminating the subsidy on gasoline and other petroleum products, on the grounds that it would improve the government's financial position while simultaneously reducing inequality. The price of gasoline in Colombia is the fourth lowest in the world and the government subsidy which permits this low price clearly is biased towards the rich. Among the urban population the richest 10 per cent consumes 40 per cent of the petroleum products while the poorest 50 per cent consumes only 18.5 per cent. In the country as a whole, the richest 10 per cent of the population consumes 11 times more petroleum products than the poorest 50 per cent of the population.[34]

There are equally numerous examples of production subsidies that benefit primarily the rich. Subsidies to agricultural inputs are particularly important. In countries which adopted 'green revolution' technology – higher-yielding seeds, chemical fertilisers, pesticides and intensive irrigation – expansion of production often became heavily dependent on input subsidies, especially to fertiliser and irrigation, and these subsidies, in turn, became a heavy burden on the exchequer, absorbing funds that might have been used to promote other forms of development in the rural areas.

In India, for example, fertiliser subsidies are huge (Rs 60 billion) and are larger than the combined central and state expenditures on agriculture. The benefits of subsidies to fertiliser, power and irrigation have been captured by medium and large farmers who have come increasingly to rely on subsidies to sustain their prosperity and have in fact organised themselves into a powerful political lobby to agitate for their continuation. The large farmers are able to capture the benefits of the subsidies precisely because they are large, i.e. because they own the land and other productive assets needed to engage in agriculture. The land in India is unequally distributed – 8 per cent of rural households own half the cultivated area – and it is this small minority that is in a good position to benefit from input subsidies.[35] The situation is similar in Bangladesh, both as regards the unequal distribution of land and the beneficiaries of fertiliser subsidies. In 1990 farmers paid 35 per cent less than the border price for potash and 30 per cent less for superphosphate. The subsidies received by farmers in the form of lower prices, however, accounted for only 44 per cent of total fertiliser subsidies. The remaining 56 per cent was used to subsidise state fertiliser producers and distributors. That is, fertiliser subsidies in Bangladesh were captured partly by medium and large farmers and partly by inefficient producers in the state enterprise sector.[36] It is unlikely that this represented the best use of public funds.

In many developing countries, government-financed irrigation schemes have benefited large farmers and bypassed small ones. This is transparently the case in Mexico, where between 1940 and 1960 the ejidos of southern Mexico were largely ignored while the government channelled huge amounts of public funds into massive irrigation projects in the northern states of Baja California, Sinaloa, Sonora and Tamaulipas. Irrigation water from these projects was provided at subsidised prices to the large farmers who acquired land there. In India, discriminatory water rates from government irrigation schemes have accentuated regional inequalities, with extremely low charges for irrigation in the rich agricultural states of Punjab, Tamil Nadu and Andhra Pradesh. In the Punjab, for instance, charges for irrigation water are only about one per cent of gross value added. If water charges were raised considerably, there would be incentives to use scarce water resources more efficiently, to protect the environment and to economise on the country's natural capital. In addition, higher water charges would contribute to greater regional equality and possibly thereby reduce political tensions created by perceptions of regional inequity. Finally, higher water charges would eliminate a subsidy to the rich and make resources available that could be used to finance human development.[37]

In addition to direct subsidies to inputs, many governments have provided indirect subsidies by providing farmers with highly-subsidised credit. The most glaring example of this occurred in Brazil during the 1970s. By the middle of that decade government-supplied agricultural credit had grown to such an extent that it was almost equal to the total gross value of agricultural output. The interest rate charged for this credit was 15 per cent a year. Given that the rate of inflation was 40–50 per cent a year, the real rate of interest for agricultural credit was highly negative, say, –25 to –35 per cent. Those who were able to obtain credit at these rates enjoyed an enormous subsidy and, as should by now be familiar, only a small proportion of Brazil's farmers were in fact given access. Eighty per cent of the farmers had no access to formal credit markets but had to rely instead on informal sources of finance. Of the remaining 20 per cent, most of the formal sector agricultural credit was given to the richest 3–4 per cent of landowners, usually in the form of very large loans. The Gini coefficient of crop loans – a measure of the degree of inequality in the distribution of credit – rose dramatically from 0.60 in 1969 to 0.71 in 1979. Income inequality in the rural areas also increased sharply during this period and the highly unequal distribution of agricultural credit undoubtedly contributed to this.[38]

The size of the subsidies mentioned above and the concentration of the subsidies on such a small fraction of the population represent both a problem and an opportunity. The problem is that government subsidies help to create and then perpetuate great inequalities in the distribution of income and wealth. Subsidies, that is, have not been used to alleviate poverty but to accentuate inequality. The magnitude of the subsidies suggests, however, that there is great scope for promoting human development through a radical reallocation of public expenditure. In many countries a government committed to human development need not raise additional revenue through taxation; it can at least begin by using the resources at hand more sensibly. The greater is the misuse of public revenues, the greater are the possibilities for bringing about significant improvements in the wellbeing of people by ending that misuse. This is the challenge and the opportunity governments face.

SUMMARY

One way of thinking about the allocation of public sector resources is in terms of a set of ratios which decompose expenditure on human development (expressed as a percentage of gross national product) into three parts: total public expenditure as a percentage of gross national product (PE/GNP); expenditure on the social sectors as a percentage of public expenditure (SS/PE); and expenditure on human development as a percentage of social sector expenditure (HD/SS). We thus have

$$HD/GNP \equiv PE/GNP \times SS/PE \times HD/SS.[39]$$

As with any tautology, the above equation is true by definition and can provide only limited insights. Moreover, the equation can be very misleading in that it implies that human development expenditures are merely a

64   *Implementing A Human Development Strategy*

subset of expenditure on the social services as a whole. We argue, in contrast, that expenditure on human development encompasses much more than the social services and includes such things as guaranteed employment schemes designed to increase the stock of physical capital. Beyond this, the equation implies that all human development expenditure is financed by government out of taxation or borrowing. This clearly is neither desirable nor a correct statement of fact. Notwithstanding these qualifications the equation does enable policymakers to explore various ways of attaining broad human development expenditure objectives.

Suppose, for example, that in a particular country the government decided that 5 per cent of the national income should be spent on human development activities (narrowly defined) financed by the public sector. One way to achieve this objective would be (i) to raise sufficient revenue to finance a public expenditure programme equivalent to 25 per cent of GNP (PE/GNP = 0.25); (ii) to allocate 20 per cent of public expenditure to the social sector (SS/PE = 0.20) and (iii) to ensure that all social sector expenditure is directed toward human development activities, defined narrowly as those concerned with primary health care and basic education (HD/SS = 1.0). This pattern of spending would enable the government to meet the target (0.5 = 0.25 × 0.20 × 1.0). Equally, the target would be met by raising PE/GNP to 30 per cent and SS/PE to 50 per cent while reducing HD/SS to 33 per cent. An infinity of combinations is possible.

In Table 3.1 we present the actual expenditure ratios for two countries in 1988. Costa Rica was selected to represent countries which give relatively high priority to human development whereas Pakistan represents countries which give low priority to human development. The weighted average of 25 developing countries also is presented.

Table 3.1   Public spending on primary health care and basic education, 1988
(percentages)

	Costa Rica	*Pakistan*	*Weighted average of 25 countries*
PE/GNP	41	25	28
SS/PE	50	21	28
HD/SS	26	14	38
HD/GNP	5.4	0.8	2.9

Source: UNDP, *Human Development Report 1991*, Table 3.1, p. 41.

Costa Rica differs from the average developing country by having a relatively large public sector and by allocating a high proportion of public expenditure to the social sector. Within the social sector it allocates less than the average to primary health care and basic education. That is, Costa Rica does not spend an exceptionally high proportion of public funds on human development as here defined; it simply has more funds to spend. Consequently, it has a high HD/GNP ratio of 5.4 per cent. Pakistan, in contrast, has a very low HD/GNP ratio of only 0.8 per cent. This is because its public expenditure ratio is lower than the average, its allocations to the social sector are smaller than average and, most striking, the proportion of social sector spending directed to primary health care and basic education is little more than a third of the average. Pakistan evidently falls short on all three ratios.

The simple identity thus has its uses as a tool of analysis. The equation cannot, of course, provide answers as to how public sector resources should be allocated, but it does raise questions which policymakers have to address. If the ratios are handled with care, they can be used to construct a rough framework for analysis and perhaps also to frame the terms for public debate.

4 Target-Setting versus a Calculus of Benefits and Costs

We have advocated above that expenditures on human development should be based in part on a calculus of benefits and costs. We are, of course, aware that it often is difficult to measure accurately the benefits of investing in people – the costs are relatively easy – but none the less we believe that all investment projects, be they additions to the stock of human, physical or natural capital, should be subjected to similar scrutiny and should be required to pass the same test. The intellectual discipline required by a calculus of benefits and costs forces analysts to make hidden assumptions explicit, enables policymakers to compare on an equal basis the alternative uses of public funds and can help prevent a waste of scare investment resources. Whether the decision rule is a benefit–cost ratio greater than one, or a positive net present value or an internal rate of return greater than a predetermined value is a secondary matter. The important thing is that a genuine effort be made to calculate benefits and costs rather than rely on intuition, common sense or political expediency.

The alternative approach, common in international circles as well as in individual countries, is to set specific targets and then, in effect, attempt to minimise the cost of attaining the target. The United Nations, for example, has elaborated an 'international development strategy' for each of the last four decades, beginning with the 1960s. The international development strategies specified global or universal targets that set identical standards for all countries regardless of circumstances, e.g. 'free education at all levels'. Moreover, the targets became increasingly numerous, rising from four in the first Development Decade (the 1960s) to more than 23 in the third Development Decade (the 1980s). Finally, the targets became increasingly ambitious and even unrealistic. For example, the growth target for the 1960s was 5 per cent; in the 1970s it was raised to 6 per cent; and in the 1980s it was raised again to 7 per cent. Actual rates of growth diverged increasingly from the targets.

Targets tend to proliferate because they specify levels of specific benefits desired – rates of growth, levels of literacy, extent of health coverage,

66

school enrolment rates, degree of industrialisation, share of world trade, etc. – and there is no limit to the number of good things that can be desired. Similarly, targets tend to be excessively ambitious because there is nothing in the process of target-setting that forces planners to estimate the cost of meeting the target. Target-setting, in other words, does not require planners to compare alternative goals and to weigh the benefits against the costs.

It is often implicitly assumed when setting a target that the unit cost is constant. In the case of a mass literacy campaign, for instance, it is assumed that the additional or marginal cost (MC) of providing literacy is independent of the size of the programme. The unit cost (or cost per person included in the programme) is the same whether the programme aims for universal adult literacy or, say, aims at a more modest target of only 80 per cent of the eligible population. This assumption is depicted in Figure 4.1(a).

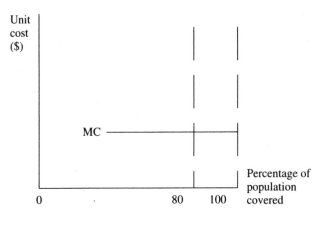

Figure 4.1(a)

In practice, however, unit costs are likely to rise as the size of the programme expands. And as one approaches complete coverage of the eligible population, the marginal cost may rise sharply. Returning to the case of a mass literacy campaign, some individuals may be more strongly motivated than others and hence may put more effort into learning to read and write, some groups (e.g. the young as compared to the elderly) may be able to learn more quickly and easily than others, and some people (e.g. those living in remote locations) may be more difficult to reach than others. If so, the marginal cost curve of a mass literacy campaign will begin after a point to rise, as depicted in Figure 4.1(b).

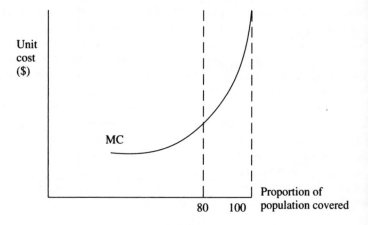

Figure 4.1(b)

In Figure 4.1(b) the marginal cost more than doubles when the literacy campaign is enlarged from 80 per cent coverage to universal coverage. As a result, the total cost of the campaign rises more than proportionately. Policymakers in circumstances such as these should ask themselves whether it is worthwhile aiming for 100 per cent coverage, or whether instead the extra funds needed to achieve universal adult literacy would be better spent on some other programme, such as a programme to reduce the infant mortality rate.

The answer depends on the expected benefits of the additional expenditure. Once again, it is often implicitly assumed when setting a target that the marginal benefits (MB) are high and constant, easily exceeding the marginal costs. On this assumption it clearly is worthwhile to aim for universal coverage. This is the situation depicted in Figure 4.2(a).

It is not difficult to imagine, however, that just as marginal costs tend to rise as coverage increases, so marginal benefits tend to fall. Some people need literacy skills more than others to earn a living; some people obtain more pleasure from leisure reading than others; some people in the early stages of life will benefit longer from the possession of literacy skills than those who are well past the prime of life. For all these reasons the benefits on the margin of expanding the coverage of a mass literacy campaign are likely to decline. This is the situation depicted in Figure 4.2(b).

Note that in Figure 4.2(b), if the target is set at universal adult literacy, the marginal costs will exceed the marginal benefits. Total benefits from the programme will be greater than total costs, but the last dollars spent will

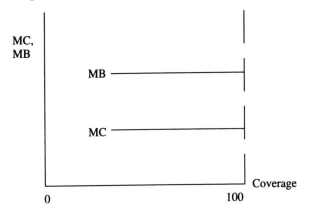

Figure 4.2(a)

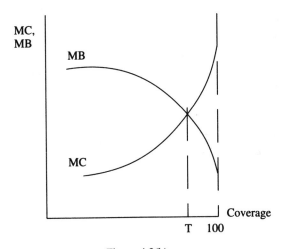

Figure 4.2(b)

have been wasted: they yielded fewer benefits than costs. The optimal size of the programme occurs where marginal benefits and costs are equal. This is point T in the figure. At this point net total benefits, i.e. total benefits minus total costs, are at a maximum and any additional resources that might become available would be better spent on some other programme. A target of T, rather than universal adult literacy, would therefore be ideal.

Target-setting, in other words, is not incompatible with a calculus of benefits and costs. Targets have their virtues – they are clear, easy to understand and can be used to mobilise public support – and these virtues can be preserved, but the targets should be set after the benefits and costs have been calculated and not plucked arbitrarily out of thin air. If the targets are set where net total benefits are maximised, policymakers can have the best of both worlds.

5 Structural Reforms

In Chapter 2 we emphasised the importance for human development of the set of incentives, i.e. of ensuring that price-signals accurately reflect costs and benefits, of guaranteeing access to markets to everyone on equal terms and of lowering barriers to entry where there is discrimination. In Chapter 3 we underlined the role of government in achieving human development objectives and emphasised the large potential gains that could be realised by a reallocation of public expenditure. In a few countries improvements in incentives and in the composition of government spending will suffice, but in most developing countries these are necessary steps that will have to be reinforced by structural reforms and institutional changes.

In this chapter we focus on a small number of structural reforms: guaranteed employment, an equitable distribution of productive assets, food security and nutrition, and economic security and welfare. These structural reforms are not substitutes for reforms of incentives and government spending; they are complementary to them. In combination they should go a long way toward ensuring that all members of society have opportunities to fulfill their potential as human beings.

The structural reforms singled out for discussion have been carefully selected. In some sense they are fundamental, for if everyone capable of productive work has an opportunity of employment, if all households have a share in society's productive assets, if every child, woman and man is assured of enough food to sustain an active life and if the lame, the sick and the infirm are entitled to a minimum of economic security, then it can truly be said that a basis exists for rapid and sustained human development. This does not imply that in some countries other reforms, such as a reform of the system of governance, may not merit higher priority, and to that extent our list should be regarded as illustrative only, but the issues raised here are ones which every society sooner or later must confront.

GUARANTEED EMPLOYMENT

Employment is fundamental to a human development strategy. Employment provides people with a source of income, it contributes to the output of goods and services and it gives workers a sense of dignity by enabling

71

them to participate in the activities of the community and to contribute something of value.[1] Equally important, employment is necessary to reap the full benefits of investment in human capital. The returns to human development expenditure will fall dramatically if those who embody human capital are unable to put their energy, skills, knowledge and initiative to productive use.

Well-conceived macroeconomic policies can help to create an economic environment conducive to rapid employment creation and a higher average productivity of labour. The structure of incentives, discussed in Chapter 2, obviously has a role to play. Three things are worth a special mention here. First, it is important that policymakers ensure that there is a positive real rate of interest in the formal sector capital markets so that borrowers have an incentive to substitute abundant labour for scarce capital. Second, an overvalued exchange rate should be avoided so that there is no incentive to substitute imported foreign equipment for domestic labour. Third, obstacles to the smooth functioning of the labour market should be removed, including the elimination of discrimination against women and other groups, the removal of all barriers to entry into markets and the weakening of factors which restrict access.

These microeconomic policies have obvious implications for the volume of employment. In addition, there are trade and budgetary policies. We have placed considerable emphasis on the importance of grasping global opportunities and the role a human development strategy can play in making this possible. Of course, the opportunities must be there to be grasped and the international environment for job-creation must be favourable. The developed countries, which dominate global trade, have clear responsibilities for maintaining an open trading system and a buoyant world economy. Given the international environment, however, it is up to the government of each developing country to ensure that its trade regime encourages an efficient use of the country's existing human capital and provides encouragement to further human capital formation. This can usually best be done by exploiting actual and potential comparative advantages in employment-intensive and human-capital-intensive activities. In addition, the government should manage its budget in such a way that the pressure of aggregate demand on total available resources is neither so great as to cause rampant inflation nor so small as to cause excess productive capacity, depressed investment incentives and open or disguised unemployment of labour. These are the core employment policies and other policies and programmes discussed below should be regarded as supplementing where necessary these core policies.

Beyond macroeconomic policies and the structure of incentives, the expenditure policies of the state are important. First, the need to create employment should be taken into account when determining the composition of expenditure. Some activities are inherently more capital-intensive than others – for example, air transport is more capital-intensive than secondary education – and differences in employment intensity should be considered when allocating resources among various activities. It fortunately is the case that those government activities which promote human development – discussed in Chapter 3 – often are relatively labour-intensive and hence there is no conflict between the need to choose an appropriate composition of public expenditure and the need to generate employment.

Second, in cases where government departments and state enterprises are insulated from market forces, steps should be taken to ensure that methods of production reflect the real cost of labour and are not excessively mechanised. This point applies in a great many fields where there is some choice among alternative techniques. Examples include construction, materials handling, transport, irrigation. Third, it is equally important that in countries which have a large public sector investment programme, the criteria used to evaluate public sector investment projects take account of the opportunity cost of labour and the desirability of generating employment. Especially in projects financed by foreign aid, capital may be underpriced and a strong implicit bias against labour may inadvertently be introduced. The same problem can arise when funds to finance state investment projects are raised through taxation and allocated through administrative and budgetary processes. The implicit price of capital may appear to the implementing agency or ministry to be low or even zero, since it is allocated a lump sum as part of a project budget, and hence a strong bias against the employment of labour may be introduced.

In a large majority of developing countries the future growth of employment will originate in the private sector and much of this will be concentrated in small-scale enterprises, whether in the informal sector or not. Particular attention should therefore be paid to ensuring that small enterprises are able to exploit their potential to the maximum. The future of employment lies not with the private oligopolies and large state monopolies that dominate the formal sector but with household enterprises and small, privately-owned firms and cooperatives in the urban and rural areas. The microeconomic policies mentioned above clearly are relevant here. In addition, the government should do what it can to remove any administrative obstacles – licenses, regulations, discriminatory taxes, city ordinances, police harassment – which prevent the expansion of household enterprises and other small businesses. Beyond this, it may be possible to provide positive assistance in the form of improved access to credit (but not a preferential interest rate), training and short courses (for example, in book-keeping) and marketing (perhaps by helping to organise marketing cooperatives). A bit of imagination and experimentation will be required, but the payoff to a successful initiative could be high.

Even if all these measures were adopted, however, the employment situation might be so serious, and the role of employment in a human development strategy so important, that a major structural reform in the form of a guaranteed employment scheme should be considered. There is nothing particularly novel about this. Many governments have experimented with public works projects as a way to reduce seasonal or year-round unemployment while creating useful assets.[2] In China the mobilisation of surplus labour within the commune system – disbanded after 1978 – was a key mechanism for rural capital construction which succeeded in large part in transforming the countryside.[3] And in the state of Maharashtra, India, a successful employment guarantee scheme has been in operation in the rural areas since 1975.[4] In Bangladesh there has been a large food-for-work programme for about three decades and in the second half of the 1980s it provided approximately 15 days of work per year for households which owned less than 0.5 acres of land.[5]

The point of departure of an employment guarantee scheme is recognition of the right of everyone to work, i.e. to guaranteed employment for performing unskilled manual labour. This right applies to women as well as men, to those who reside in urban as well as rural areas, and to all able-bodied persons aged, say, 15 or above. A programme for guaranteed employment would thus be open to anyone who applied. It would in effect act as the residual source of employment and would place a safety net under those most in need. The wage rate would be the same for women and men, although some regional variation could be introduced if the price of wage goods differed substantially from one part of the country to another or between rural and urban areas.

The programme should concentrate on the construction of productive assets, including investments in infrastructure projects, that can be expected in future to contribute to sustained higher levels of output and income. That is, the guaranteed employment programme should not be regarded as a short-term measure to provide relief in an emergency or during a period of readjustment and restructuring; nor should it be regarded as an income transfer or welfare programme. Rather, it should be seen as a mechanism for mobilising otherwise unused resources for capital formation and growth. It is thus a component of a long-term human development strategy, and the employment scheme should be closely integrated into the government's overall policy framework.

In areas where unemployment is chronic, particularly in some urban areas, it may be necessary to organise the scheme on a permanent, year-round basis. In many rural areas, however, the problem of unemployment is largely seasonal and the employment guarantee scheme would have to be designed to mesh into the agricultural cycle and supplement normal earnings from crop cultivation. But whether seasonal or permanent, the programme should emphasise labour-intensive, low-cost infrastructure and other capital construction projects. Obvious candidates include small-scale irrigation works, soil conservation, afforestation and orchard planting, housing and water supply, construction of primary schools and primary health stations, rural roads. The creation of assets intended to raise future incomes should be a primary objective.

(i) The Wage Rate

Any able-bodied person seeking employment and willing to do manual work should be guaranteed a job at a subsistence wage. The daily wage rate or piece rate should be set at a level which does not attract workers from other jobs, since the purpose of the scheme is to provide work to those who have no other source of gainful employment. In the rural areas this means that the wage should be set marginally below, say 10 per cent below, the wages received by hired agricultural workers in the lowest-income regions of the country. Such a wage probably would reflect fairly closely the opportunity cost of labour and would allay any fears that the guaranteed employment scheme would raise labour costs and damage employment prospects in other sectors of the economy.

Projects should be designed in such a way that labour costs account for a high proportion of the total. As a guideline, one might aim for projects in which the costs of employment represent about two-thirds or more of total project costs. The experience of Maharashtra indicates this is realistic. If, for any reason, work cannot be provided to those who seek it, and the government is in fact unable to guarantee employment, unemployment compensation should be paid at a rate equivalent to the daily wage rate on works projects. This will provide an incentive to government to design and implement useful projects since, if they do not, the workers will be entitled to a wage payment in any case.

(ii) Financing the Programme

In a macroeconomic sense the programme should be self-financing in the long run, since if the investment projects are selected carefully they should generate a stream of future benefits, the discounted value of which exceeds the costs of construction. Nevertheless there may be a problem of public finance if the government is unable to cover its outlays through taxation of either the additional income generated or the additional wealth created. In the rural areas, costs could be recovered through a tax on land and in the urban areas through a value-added tax on transactions. In practice, however, it is unlikely to be possible to ensure that the ultimate beneficiaries bear the full tax burden. This programme, like virtually all government activities whether related to human development or not, will have to be financed out of general government revenues, national or provincial.

The difficulty of doing so should not be exaggerated. The large employment guarantee scheme in Maharashtra, for example, accounts for only 8 per cent of total state expenditure. It thus comes down to a question of priorities. If the provision of employment to all is sufficiently important, it should be possible either to raise additional public revenue or to reallocate public expenditure from low-priority to high-priority activities.

(iii) Distribution of the Benefits

If a guaranteed employment programme is a success, a number of valuable assets will be created. These assets will raise both rural and urban land values and hence the incomes and general wellbeing of those who own the land. Since the landholders will in virtually all countries be better off to begin with than the unskilled and otherwise unemployed labourers who work at subsistence wages to create the assets, the effect of the employment programme, paradoxically, could well be to increase inequalities in the distribution of income and wealth. This clearly would be an unintended consequence of the programme and specific remedies should be introduced to counter it.

The workers who participate would receive two types of benefits from an employment scheme. First, they would receive subsistence wages during the period when the work is undertaken. In Maharashtra more than three-quarters of the beneficiaries are landless workers or small farmer households; about 40 per cent of those employed are women. The subsistence wages in some cases account for between one-third and two-thirds of total household incomes. Thus the direct benefits accrue largely to the poor and are not negligible when seen from their perspective.

Second, to the extent that the assets created under the scheme generate a permanently higher demand for labour, the workers should enjoy in future some combination of higher market wage rates and more employment opportunities. Most of the benefits, however, are likely to accrue to land-owners in the form of lower costs (e.g. if farm-to-market roads lower the cost of transport), higher yields (e.g. from irrigation projects), higher land rents and hence higher land prices. Moreover, the benefits to landowners are likely to vary more than proportionately with the size of holding. This would occur, for instance, if a project lowers transport costs and the market-able surplus increases with the size of farm.

One way to overcome the problem of an unequal distribution of benefits would be to impose a progressive land tax. A more imaginative way would be to transfer ownership of the assets created by unemployed workers to the workers themselves. This could readily be done by forming a multi-purpose cooperative or worker-managed enterprise, the shares in which would be proportional to the number of days worked on the construction projects. The cooperative would then be responsible for maintaining the assets, managing them and distributing profits among the shareholder-cooperators. Unem-ployed workers would thereby gradually be converted into asset-holders, although they should be free to cash in their shares with the cooperative if they wished.

Not all assets created by the employment programme could be managed in this way, but considerable scope exists for simultaneously transforming idle labour into physical capital and workers into shareholders in coopera-tive enterprises. The impetus this would give to human development could be quite considerable. For example, a cooperative could be organised around an irrigation project and water sold to farmers; a timber, firewood or fruit cooperative could be organised around a tree-planting project; a toll-charging company could be organised around a bridge-building project; a fishing or duck cooperative could be based on an artificial pond, and so on. These individual cooperatives could then be grouped into a multi-purpose cooperative that would have overall responsibility for managing the collec-tively constructed assets. Such an approach could have an enormous impact – provided, of course, that the projects are selected carefully.

(iv) Project Selection

The projects selected for a guaranteed employment programme should ideally satisfy several criteria. First, we have already emphasised that they should be highly labour-intensive, since a primary purpose of the scheme is to act as the residual source of employment for those who otherwise would be unemployed and without an income. Second, again as previously empha-sised, the projects should result in the creation of permanent assets which can raise future output and incomes. Third, whenever possible, the projects should be located near the homes of the workers, be they residents of rural or urban areas. Fourth, in so far as possible, the projects should form the nucleus of a cooperative or workers' enterprise to ensure that the benefits of the project accrue largely to those who work on it. Alternatively, fifth, projects should be located in areas where local organisations of peasants and workers already exist which can take responsibility for the management and maintenance of the assets created. That is, the projects should be used to encourage participation of the otherwise unemployed and to empower them.[6] Finally, failing this, projects should be located in areas of the coun-tryside or parts of cities where the distribution of land ownership is rela-tively equal.

If these criteria of selection are satisfied, a guaranteed employment programme should be able to reduce unemployment substantially, alleviate poverty in the short run by providing a subsistence income to those most in need, contribute to a faster rate of growth by creating productive assets and, in the long run, improve the distribution of income and the ownership of productive wealth. In addition, an employment scheme can serve as a catalyst for institutional change, facilitating participation at the local level in economic affairs and empowering those who at present are the poorest and have the least amount of power.

(v) Administration

Overall financial administration obviously will have to be the responsibility of the central or a provincial government, from where the funds presumably will originate. Selection and implementation of projects, however, should occur at the local level. Those seeking employment should have designated places at which to register, near to where they live, and it would then be the responsibility of the local authorities to provide employment within, say, two weeks. If no work is offered within that period, the local authorities would be required, as suggested above, to pay all registered workers an unemployment allowance. This would provide an incentive to the authori-ties to make certain that work is in fact offered, since in any event they would have to pay labour costs, and it would also make certain that the poor receive a subsistence income even if the authorities are unable to provide productive employment.

The projects themselves could be implemented by the local government, by peasant organisations, by trade unions or by other non-governmental organisations. The objective should be to involve as many institutions as possible in the identification and design of suitable employment-creating projects and in the actual organisation of the work. The only condition should be that those entrusted to implement the programme are technically competent to undertake labour-intensive investment projects. A monitoring system should be introduced by the local authorities to prevent corruption and misuse of funds.

The guaranteed employment scheme could perhaps begin on a small scale, as an experiment. Once experience is gained, it should then be extended to the entire country. The results of such schemes in the two largest developing countries, China and India, indicate that they can contribute a great deal to human development. It is likely that many other countries can gain from the experience of China and India and apply the lessons to their own specific conditions.

THE DISTRIBUTION OF PRODUCTIVE ASSETS

Even if everyone seeking a job is able to obtain productive employment, the pace of human development is likely to be very slow if the distribution of income-generating wealth is highly unequal. The reason for this is that the flow of income originates from the stock of natural, physical and human capital. Even if human capital is spread fairly evenly across the entire population, e.g. because of public provision of essential services such as education, health, sanitation and clean water, income as a whole will be distributed unequally, and human development frustrated, if the ownership of natural and physical capital is concentrated in a few hands. A household's income depends on the amount of capital it possesses (human, natural and physical) and on the rate of return earned on its capital. If the household owns neither natural nor physical capital, it will be forced to rely entirely on its income from human capital. Experience throughout the developing world demonstrates that in most cases this is not enough to prevent large numbers of people falling into poverty.

The connection between poverty and the distribution of wealth is seen most vividly in the rural areas. The poorest of the poor almost always are members of households that are assetless. Indeed the absence of productive assets is a sure sign of poverty, often dire poverty. Landlessness usually is the primary cause of economic distress in the countryside, but landlessness typically goes hand-in-hand with an absence of other productive assets,

namely, livestock, implements and other equipment, barns and other immovable assets. Particularly in Latin America and parts of Asia, landownership tends to be highly concentrated and the large landowners tend to
possess most of the other productive assets as well. It is hardly surprising
that many of the great agrarian rebellions of the twentieth century
have occurred in these two regions: Mexico and Bolivia, China and the
Philippines.

In countries which have not had a sweeping agrarian reform, poverty and
income inequality are closely associated with inequality in the distribution
of land. In Bangladesh, for instance, small farms (those up to 2.5 acres in
size) account for 70 per cent of all farms, yet small farms account for only
29 per cent of the cultivated land. At the other extreme, farms over 10 acres
in size account for only 5 per cent of all farms but 26 per cent of all land.[7]
The distribution of land in the other countries of South Asia is broadly
similar. In India in 1982, two-thirds of all farms were an acre or less, yet
they accounted for only 6 per cent of the cultivated land; 11 per cent of the
farms were larger than 15 acres and they accounted for 61 per cent of the
land.[8] In Pakistan, landownership is heavily concentrated: in 1976 farms
larger than 50 acres accounted for 58 per cent of the land in the Sind
province and about 82 per cent of the land in the Punjab, the richest
province in the country.[9]

Self-reliant human development in the rural areas can often be achieved
most quickly through the careful design and implementation of a land
reform. A redistribution of property rights in land and water, accompanied
as necessary by technical assistance, credit to small farmers and improved
marketing, is very likely to improve allocative efficiency[10] as well as the
distribution of income, and there is no evidence that it reduces the long-term
rate of growth of agricultural output. Indeed, the experience in Asia and
elsewhere indicates that rapid agricultural growth does not necessarily lead
to higher incomes of the very poor or to human development in general, and
where growth has been translated into higher incomes of the poor, the
incomes of the non-poor usually have risen relatively faster, with the result
that inequality has increased. The reason that the benefits of growth do not
reach the poor or fail to reach them in full measure is that landless labourers,
tenant farmers and small peasant cultivators participate only marginally in
the benefits of technical change, the source of long-run agricultural growth.
Their lack of productive assets means that at best they have only a weak link
with growth-generating mechanisms (e.g. investments in physical and natural capital) and because of their high dependence on the remuneration of
labour for their livelihood, they do not share in the higher profits and rents
that accompany growth.

In principle, it is possible to imagine massive and sustained state intervention intended to compensate the poor for their lack of productive assets. Policies to redistribute income, provide health and education services, mother and child care programmes, and ensure adequate nutrition, etc. obviously have a role to play – as we have argued repeatedly – but they cannot be expected to carry the full burden of great inequality in the distribution of wealth. First, the costs would be too high, for in effect the state would be attempting to compensate for the inability of large segments of the rural population to provide for themselves. Second, as long as the distribution of productive assets is unequal, the distribution of primary incomes will be unequal and those who receive the larger portion of the primary incomes can be expected continuously to resist government efforts to redistribute part of their income to others via taxation. We have already seen that the rich resist, often successfully, the removal of handsome subsidies that favour them. They will resist even more strongly attempts to take away part of their income. Thus on political as well as economic grounds there is a case for a once-for-all redistribution of assets.

Land reform, in particular, is likely to accelerate human development because of its effects on agricultural production and the employment of labour. Output per hectare tends to be higher on small farms than on large, because small farmers use their land more intensively (have a higher cropping ratio) and utilise more labour-intensive techniques of production. A redistribution of large landholdings in favour of the landless and those with very small holdings will bring about not only a more equitable distribution of income but also a higher level of income and output. In addition, because small farmers economise on land and physical capital relative to labour, employment per hectare also should increase. Thus two of the major causes of rural poverty, namely landlessness and underemployment, can be largely overcome by a comprehensive land reform.

In some countries water reform is almost as important as land reform. State-owned tube wells could be 'privatized' by turning them over to groups of landless people who would then have the right to pump and sell irrigation water and the responsibility to maintain the wells and pumps. The beneficiaries could be organised into cooperatives similar to those recommended for the management of assets created under guaranteed employment schemes. One local non-governmental organisation has experimented with such an arrangement in Bangladesh and its experience has demonstrated that the idea is viable. With a bit of imagination it might be possible to design similar arrangements for the management and control of surface waters, thereby redistributing the ownership of part of the natural stock of capital to those who possess few productive assets.

It is sometimes argued that because of high population densities in some countries, the amount of land potentially available for redistribution is so limited that a land reform is not worthwhile. This view is not correct: whenever landownership is highly unequal there are gains to be had from redistribution, although where land is in very short supply it might be argued that cooperative or communal forms of organisation become relatively more attractive. Even where land–man ratios are exiguous, however, human development can be advanced in rural areas by allocating to each family at least enough land to erect a house, cultivate a kitchen garden of vegetables and fruit and raise small livestock (chickens, ducks, pigs, rabbits). This is the bare minimum to which everyone should be entitled.

Where economies of scale can be exploited, small farmers should be encouraged and assisted to develop institutional arrangements – mutual aid societies, specialised cooperatives, irrigation associations, communes, etc. – which enable them to pool resources and undertake activities at the most efficient scale of operation. As we have seen earlier in this chapter, the most valuable asset of the poor often is their own labour power, and rural employment programmes can mobilise seasonally-available labour to create new physical and natural capital – irrigation and drainage facilities, earth roads and dams, small bridges, and land improvements such as hillside terraces, orchards and fuel wood planting projects. In many cases the assets created could become the property, individual or collective, of those whose labour created them. This would have the advantage of providing a permanent source of income for the poor and an incentive to protect that source of income through regular repair and maintenance of the asset. Apart from pooling labour, small farmers can join together to purchase and operate agricultural machinery that is too costly for an individual farmer and requires a larger area for efficient operation than is typical of a small farm. Such machinery cooperatives can help to raise the productivity of labour by overcoming any diseconomies of small plots that may arise. Similarly, credit and marketing cooperatives may have a role to play in supplementing the services offered by the private sector.

Land reform has been most successful in countries such as Japan, China, South Korea and Taiwan province, China where the rural population is well-organised and is able to implement the reform after it has been adopted as national policy. Thus the experience of land reform is consistent with a wider proposition that informs this analysis, namely, that human development proceeds most rapidly when the people concerned participate fully in the process. In the specific case of land reform, participation is critical for success since land reform is impossible unless it is accompanied by a change in the balance of political forces. Once land reform has been implemented, the beneficiaries – landless labourers, tenant cultivators and small owner-operators – should be encouraged to create new institutions which permit them to play an active role in economic affairs and in the political life of the community.

Among capitalist economies, Taiwan and South Korea are notable for putting priority on a redistribution of productive assets before the growth of output. In both cases a land reform was the key redistributive measure. In Taiwan the land reform occurred between 1949 and 1953. Nearly a quarter of the cultivated land was transferred to the poorest 48 per cent of the rural population and this redistribution was equivalent to about 13 per cent of Taiwan's gross national product at the time.[11]

The land reform in Taiwan was comprehensive and led to the creation of an egalitarian small peasant farming system. The degree of local participation in the reform process was high: authority to implement the reforms was entrusted to each village and farmers were encouraged by the government to form associations to provide credit, storage, marketing and extension services. In addition, irrigation cooperatives were formed so that farmers could manage the irrigation systems that served them. As a result of all this, a considerable degree of economic democracy prevailed at the local level, although the national regime was politically authoritarian. The land reform, however, shaped the subsequent development trajectory in Taiwan and helped create a relatively egalitarian society, with a capacity for broadly-based human development. One indication of this is the evolution of the Gini coefficient of the distribution of household income. In 1953 it was 0.56; by 1964 it had fallen dramatically to 0.32 and it then fell further to 0.28 in 1980. Inequality then began to increase slightly, but by 1987 the Gini coefficient still was only 0.30, i.e. the distribution of income still was one of the most egalitarian in the world. Land reform contributed to this process in two ways: by removing major inequalities in the countryside, and by increasing the opportunity cost of rural labour (and hence real wages) of those who migrated from the countryside to the cities. The effect of land reform on urban wages was one of the key factors which led to a dramatic rise in the share of wages in national income.

The land reform in South Korea during the late 1940s and early 1950s was similar to that in Taiwan. Prior to the reform, landownership was highly concentrated but operational holdings were distributed fairly equally among tenants. Indeed, about half of South Korea's farmers were tenants and were effectively assetless. Thanks to the reform, 80 per cent of all land under tenancy, and virtually all land owned by absentee landlords, was transferred to small peasant farmers. The beneficiaries, in turn, were subject to an ownership ceiling: they were not allowed to possess more than three hectares of land.[12] In both South Korea and Taiwan sweeping land reform was made easier politically by the weakening of the landlord class – either because the landowners were Japanese or because indigenous landowners collaborated with the Japanese colonial authorities. When the Japanese were expelled at the end of the Second World War the landowning class found itself vulnerable to attack and without defenders. There were thus particular historical circumstances that made structural reforms possible in these two cases. Obviously the situation was and is very different in other countries. This points not to the exceptional difficulty of introducing structural change and institutional reform but to the need to consider the uniqueness of each situation and to exploit whatever opportunities exist.

Unlike Taiwan, the distribution of income in South Korea began to worsen from the mid-1960s. The main reason for this was widening income differentials between rural and urban areas. In the immediate post-land-reform period, rural incomes were roughly the same as urban, but by 1970 they were only 67 per cent as high.[13] The government responded to growing rural-urban inequality with a series of measures – greater investment in rural areas, better terms of trade for agriculture, and the launching of a New Village Movement to raise household incomes and improve living conditions in the countryside.

But South Korea's problem of rising inequality between the cities and the countryside has occurred in many other countries that have experienced industrialisation and rapid growth. This common problem suggests that one should take a broad view of the redistribution of productive assets. Development policy often has concentrated on promoting industrial expansion, with the result that agriculture has been severely under-capitalised, the countryside has lacked basic physical infrastructure (roads, power, communications) and rural development has withered for lack of finance. The outcome often has been deprivation, poverty and an absence of human development in the countryside. If human development is to become a reality in the rural areas, governments must reverse their policies, stop the squeeze on agriculture and stem the flow of capital from the countryside. This will require a substantial redistribution of effort and of public investment in favour of rural areas. The social rates of return on such investments in natural, physical and human capital are likely to be high.

The land reform introduced in China, beginning in 1978, was similar in some respects to the earlier reforms in South Korea and Taiwan, although the initial conditions obviously were very different. In each case, the final outcome was an egalitarian agrarian structure centred around small peasant holdings. In the case of China, however, the reforms of the late 1970s were not a once-for-all measure but merely the latest stage in a long sequence of reforms that began in the 1940s – a sequence that included the formation of mutual aid teams, small and then large production cooperatives and the commune system. The most recent reforms included a dismantling of the communal tenure system and reorganisation of brigade and commune level enterprises. In the process of reform, some of the advantages of the commune system were lost, e.g. the pooling of labour for investment, the provision of basic services and the maintenance and expansion of some capital assets such as irrigation facilities. On the other hand, the incentive system was improved, output became more diversified and small-scale rural industry enjoyed exceptionally rapid growth. Both agricultural and industrial output increased and average household incomes in the rural areas rose dramatically.

The distribution of wealth that emerged after all these changes is remarkably equal. The Gini coefficient for the distribution of net worth in rural China was 0.31 in 1988, which surely represents one of the most equal distributions of wealth in the world.[14] The largest component of total assets, namely land, was distributed among households on an equal per capita or in a few cases on an equal per worker basis. Hence the distribution of land after the reform was extraordinarily uniform and this virtually guaranteed that the overall distribution of wealth would be egalitarian. In addition, unlike other countries, the distribution of fixed productive assets (livestock, farm and non-farm machinery and tools, buildings) actually has an equalising effect on the distribution of total assets in China. One reason for this is the way specialised economic activities have developed in the rural areas. Some households have moved out of farming in order to concentrate on industrial and service activities. They may possess little or no land or farm capital, but they do own non-agricultural assets, including their own homes. The assets of these specialised households are comparable in value to the assets of farm households, and hence marked differences in wealth between farming households and those engaged in non-farm occupations have failed to emerge. As long as this pattern persists, rural China may be able to combine an equitable distribution of wealth and income with increased diversification of production and rapid growth of total output. This, in turn, would augur well for future human development.

FOOD SECURITY

Food security is, of course, essential for life and even where there is enough food to prevent death by starvation, individuals may not consume sufficient food to enable them to lead a full life or achieve their maximum productivity. In this sense they may be undernourished. There is abundant evidence that growth alone does not necessarily result in better nutrition.[15] As in developed countries, there is in developing countries many a slip between the cup and the lip, between a rise in aggregate average incomes and an improvement in the nutritional wellbeing of the population. On the other hand, where a permanent improvement in nutrition does indeed occur, in the form of a higher weight-for-height ratio, there is evidence that this results in a higher productivity of labour and in higher wages.[16] Thus food security, and specifically adequate nutrition, is one of the ends of human development while also being a means to human development.

Let us elaborate on this point.[17] One can think of the productivity of labour (π) as depending on, among other things, the stock of human capital embodied in the worker. The larger is the stock of human capital per worker, the larger, up to a point, will be the resulting flow of output per worker. In the specific case of nutrition, human capital in the form of the nutritional status of the worker (NS) or the general health status of the worker may be one of the determinants of output. If nutritional status is below some critical level necessary to maintain the body functioning properly (M), a person will die (and of course produce no output). If nutritional status is above some other critical level (NS_{max}), output per worker will be at a maximum and any further improvement in nutritional status (however desirable it may be on other grounds) will have no effect on a worker's productivity. In between M and NS_{max}, an improvement in NS will raise π.

This relationship between π (a flow) and NS (a stock) is depicted in Figure 5.1. The curve traces the functional relationship $\pi = f(NS)$.

It is clear from Figure 5.1 that for those individuals whose nutritional status is between M and NS_{max}, an increase in nutritional status would result in higher output. Not only would such people find that their enjoyment of life and their capabilities increase, but actual physical output would rise as well. In the great majority of countries only a fraction of the population, perhaps only a small fraction, suffers from a nutritional status of less than NS_{max}. That being the case, it should be a manageable task for public policy to alter the distribution of resources in such a way that the nutritional status of every member of society is raised to at least NS_{max}.

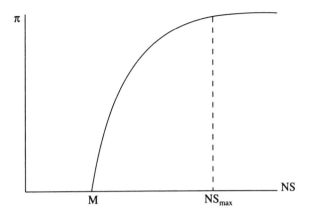

Figure 5.1

Although the task is manageable, the results will not be instantaneous. The reason for this is that π is not a function of current food intake, e.g. in the form of calorie consumption, but of the embodied stock of human capital as reflected in nutritional status, perhaps measured by cumulative calorie consumption over a number of years. The accumulation of human capital, in other words, takes time and requires sustained investment in human nutrition. The lower is a person's NS, the longer it is likely to take to raise it to NS_{max}. This suggests that the time to begin to invest in the nutritional status of people is at birth, if not before.

Assume the frequency distribution of the nutritional status of a country's population is as described in Figure 5.2 The distribution is skewed left to reflect the likelihood that there will be a significant tail of malnourished people with $NS < NS_{max}$. The population so affected is represented by the shaded area in the diagram. The nutritional status of the rest of the population, in contrast, is sufficiently good that their productivity is unaffected.

The objective of policy should be to increase the food security of the adversely affected population to prevent their nutritional status falling below the critical level of NS_{max}. This could occur either by shifting the entire frequency distribution to the right or by eliminating the left skewness in the distribution, or by a combination of the two. Policies which have this effect are likely to enjoy a high rate of return, even if the return is measured narrowly in terms of additional output produced.

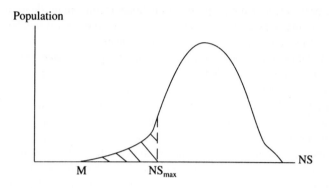

Figure 5.2

It does not follow from this, however, that food security need be an explicit objective of public policy. In principle, food security could occur as an indirect result of policies intended primarily to achieve other objectives, such as faster growth or a more equal distribution of income. Indeed, if the policies and programmes previously discussed are fully implemented – primary health care (including family planning), basic education (including health and nutrition education), guaranteed employment and a relatively equal distribution of income and wealth – then the problem of chronic food insecurity should be a relatively minor one. Growth within such a framework would be equitable; the poor would have sufficient purchasing power to enable them to acquire a nutritionally adequate diet and the problem of hunger, at worst, would be reduced to infrequent threats of famine.

Unfortunately, however, we live in a far from perfect world and governments may need to intervene to ensure that everyone has access to a minimum amount of food. The form of intervention can vary enormously – from food stamps in the United States, extensive food-rationing in China and food-supplementation schemes in Tamil Nadu, India, to food-for-work programmes in Bangladesh – and the most appropriate form of intervention will depend on a number of factors, including the nature of the nutrition problem and the range of other related policies already in place.[18] Even assuming a fairly ambitious public food distribution programme, the cost to the government need not be very large, provided the government has adopted a human development strategy and at least some of the basic components of the strategy have been implemented.

One way of estimating the costs of famine prevention, following Amartya

Sen, would be to calculate the proportion of national income required to 're-create' the income of potential famine victims so that they could purchase the amount of food necessary to prevent serious hunger. Sen argues that 'the costs of such public action for famine prevention are typically rather modest even for poor countries, provided they make systematic and efficient arrangements in good time.'[19] What these 'systematic and efficient arrangements' might be will be discussed in a moment, but first let us continue with a consideration of costs. Sen assumes, as an upper limit, that 10 per cent of the population will be potential victims of famine and, because they are the very poor, they would normally account for no more than 3 per cent of the country's gross national product. Their normal share of food consumption would be no greater than four or five per cent of the national total. 'Thus the resources needed to re-create their entire income, or to resupply their entire normal food consumption, starting from zero, do not have to be very large.'[20] Moreover, since famine victims seldom are completely wiped out but usually have some resources, the net resource requirement that will have to be provided by the government will be less than 3 per cent of GNP or 5 per cent of total food consumption. A famine prevention or food security policy thus is feasible if a sufficiently high priority is given to it.

The best way to ensure systematic and efficient arrangements for food security is to introduce a self-targeting food rationing scheme.[21] The purpose of the scheme would be to provide the entire population, in rural and urban areas, with guaranteed access to a minimum amount of a staple food (usually a foodgrain) at a price which even the poor can afford. Thus the scheme, first, would be permanent and not mounted hastily on an *ad hoc* basis during an emergency. Second, it would be universal in coverage and not restricted to particular groups identified in advance as needing public assistance. Third, the rationed staple distributed under the scheme would be sold at a subsidised price. The extent of the subsidy could vary from time to time depending on circumstances and, indeed, could fall to zero if there were no serious threat of hunger.

Fourth, the amount of the staple each individual would be entitled to purchase at a subsidised price would be determined in such a way that at the aggregate level the total of rationed supplies plus purchases obtained on the free market would cover the minimum needs for food. The quantities distributed under the scheme could vary from time to time, falling when the situation of the poor improves and increasing when the possibility of famine rises. Finally, the rationing system should in practice strongly discriminate in favour of the poor by distributing a staple food that normally is purchased predominantly by low-income groups. In practice this means supplying 'inferior' cereals, i.e. those with a negative income elasticity of demand, or staples with low-quality grades not acceptable to buyers at the top end of the market. It is this last feature of the scheme which contains the self-targeting element. Although everyone, rich and poor alike, is entitled to a given quantity of the rationed staple at a given price, only the poor are likely to take advantage of the entitlement, since it is only they who consume the staple in large quantities. Self-targeting, in other words, would help to limit the size of the programme and keep total costs low. Moreover, as growth proceeds and the incidence of poverty declines, sales of low-quality products and staples with a negative income elasticity of demand will fall, the need for food-rationing will diminish and the scheme will in effect become self-liquidating. Attention can then shift to less ambitious programmes designed to eliminate residual malnutrition in well-defined and very small groups of the population.

ECONOMIC SECURITY

Throughout this essay we have focused on two aspects of human development, namely, human development as an end in itself and human development as a means for achieving increased wellbeing. We now turn our attention briefly to a third aspect of human development, namely, its role in preventing severe deprivation. The objective in this case is protection rather than promotion. That is, the objective is to sustain people's capabilities to lead a minimally acceptable life.[22]

Individuals and families in all societies are vulnerable to unexpected events, e.g. the death of an income-earner, unemployment, sudden physical disability, incapacitating illness or destruction of a crop (by flood, drought, storm, pests) on which one's livelihood depends. People are also subject to long-term disabilities such as congenital handicaps or the infirmities of old age. The question that arises in developing countries and elsewhere is whether public policy can play a useful role in mitigating the effects of catastrophe, and if so, given the other possible claims on public resources, whether it would be wise to allocate revenues to that purpose.

It should be said straightaway that a central objective of policies to ensure economic security should be to create the conditions in which individuals and families can help themselves. The human development policies discussed earlier in this monograph do precisely that. If everyone is assured of basic health care services, food security, a job and an equitable share of the country's income and wealth, the conditions in which self-help can flourish will have been created. The residual needs for protection should be rather modest and the cost of meeting those needs rather low. Self-help combined with self-selection (in the cases of guaranteed employment and food rationing) should suffice for the great majority of people.

Some might argue that the residual economic insecurity can be left to the market for solution: no further public policy measures should be necessary. If the expected flow of people's income over time fails to coincide with the flow of desired or planned expenditure, the difference can be reconciled through the capital market. That is, people can save (or lend) their surplus funds when expenditure is less than total income and they can borrow funds during periods when income is less than desired expenditure. Thus actual expenditure can be brought into balance with 'permanent' income even in periods when 'permanent' and actual income differ. Similarly, the market can significantly reduce the consequences of catastrophe. Insurance markets, after all, are designed to cope with risk: life insurance is concerned with the risk of death, crop insurance with the risk of drought, and similarly with marine insurance, automobile insurance, earthquake insurance, unemployment insurance. Provided the credit and insurance markets function efficiently, the residual economic insecurity that remains after the basic human development policies have been put in place should be of little consequence.

The rub, however, is in the proviso. Capital markets, particularly in developing countries, work far from perfectly and it is the lowest income groups who are most vulnerable to unexpected events and who have least access to credit and insurance markets. This suggests that in the first instance measures to increase economic security should focus on the poor. That is, the poor face a case of market failure and consequently there are grounds for governments to act in effect as lender and insurer of last resort. Whether this can be done at an acceptable cost is an empirical matter to be determined in each country, but in principle the net transactions costs to government – the subsidy required out of general tax revenues – for providing residual economic security in instances of severe deprivation should be very modest indeed.

If the market cannot be relied upon to solve the problem of economic security, perhaps some might argue that the solution is economic growth. Severe deprivation has disappeared in developed countries, it might be claimed, because average incomes are high and people consequently are able to provide for themselves when unforeseen events occur. Public intervention, according to this view, is not necessary.

This view, however, is a caricature of reality. Growth in the rich countries certainly has helped reduce severe deprivation, but growth alone has not been sufficient. Public policy in the advanced capitalist and socialist countries alike, in the form of a wide range of welfare measures, has played a prominent role both in raising the wellbeing of the weakest and poorest members of society and in protecting the accustomed living standards of the population from unexpected as well as predictable declines. The achievements of the welfare state should not be underestimated.[23] Even so, deprivation remains in many rich countries such as the United States in the form of high unemployment (especially among minority groups), poverty (especially among children), hunger and lack of access to medical assistance.

Thus relatively well-functioning markets and decades of growth of per capita incomes have not eliminated the need for governments to assume some responsibility for economic security, even in very rich countries. Indeed, public expenditure on the welfare state, i.e. spending on all cash benefits plus public expenditure on health care, varies from 11.9 per cent of gross domestic product in Japan to 28.3 per cent in the Netherlands.[24] The major benefits, which, of course, vary from one country to another, are medical and sickness benefits, unemployment compensation, old-age pensions, family allowance and social assistance to the needy. These welfare programmes clearly have succeeded in reducing poverty and inequality significantly and they have thereby increased economic security. It is estimated, for example, that in Australia and the United States, two countries that spend relatively little on welfare programmes, the number of people living in poverty was reduced by 49.3 and 22.6 per cent, respectively, as a result of the tax and transfer system. In contrast, in Germany and Sweden, two high-spending countries, the reduction in poverty was 76 and 82.2 per cent, respectively.[25] Similarly, in a ranking of eight countries by the degree of inequality post-tax-and-transfer, the United States ranked as the most unequal, followed by Australia, whereas Sweden ranked as the most equal, followed by Germany.[26]

The ideal way to achieve economic security, no doubt, would be through a combination of growth and what has been called a 'social security strategy'.[27] Growth would provide the resources while the 'social security strategy' would ensure that some of these extra resources are used to reduce deprivation. The question this raises is whether developing countries can afford a social security strategy or whether, to put it slightly differently, there is a conflict between accelerating growth and providing social security. Several points can be made about this alleged conflict.

First, social security, or as we prefer to call it, economic security is an objective in itself. It is one of the ends of human development. Growth is merely one means – an important means, to be sure – towards achieving that end. Second, many of the components of a 'social security strategy' have already been discussed above and defended as efficient means of promoting growth. They are not in conflict with growth but are an integral part of a programme to accelerate growth. We refer to expenditures on primary health care, water and sanitation facilities, guaranteed employment (as an alternative to unemployment compensation), redistribution of assets (as an alternative to tax and transfer programmes designed to reduce poverty and inequality) and food security. These expenditures can be justified in a growth context because they have high rates of return, i.e. rates of return at least as high as investments in physical and natural capital.

This leaves us, then, with measures intended not to promote human development but to protect people from the vicissitudes of life. Under this category come expenditures on old-age pensions, widows' benefits, assistance to the permanently handicapped and disabled. The only potentially costly item on this list is old-age pensions. Assistance to the disabled will almost certainly be a minor item of expenditure, except in countries which have suffered high casualties in a war. Widows' benefits, too, will not be costly, since young widows will have income from a job (under the guaranteed employment programme) plus some productive assets (from the asset-redistribution programme); old widows should be entitled to a pension. Hence, the residual need to help widows is likely to be small and will consist primarily of assistance to widows with young children.

We thus are left with pensions and it is our view that developing countries should seriously consider, perhaps in stages, financing and implementing a pension scheme in which all working people participate, not just urban residents employed in the formal sector, as is often the case. The age at which women and men become eligible for a pension and the monthly payment obviously will have to reflect the demographic, economic and fiscal circumstances of the country but, in principle, it should be possible to provide a measure of economic security to the elderly even in very poor countries. If this is too ambitious in the first instance, then one can begin by providing a pension to the lowest income groups, rather than to the upper-income groups, as is almost always the case. This is our third point.

Fourth, public expenditure on a pension scheme can be justified in part on economic grounds. It is now widely recognised that one of the motives for having children is provision of economic security in old age. Children, once they become adult workers, are a form of insurance for their parents – not just insurance against the infirmities of old age, but insurance against many of the catastrophes that can occur without warning. Children, thus, are a substitute for economic security measures that protect the livelihood of people and, in particular, they are a substitute for old-age pensions. It follows from this that state-funded pension schemes in developing countries are likely to result in a reduction in the demand for children, a decline in the fertility rate and a slower rate of growth of the population. This in turn is likely to lead to a faster rate of growth of income per head. Thus measures such as pensions that are intended to increase economic security, to protect people's incomes and capabilities, also contribute indirectly to promoting human development. Protection and promotion often go hand-in-hand.

Lastly, there is the empirical observation that in fact a number of developing countries have given priority to expenditures on economic security. Among the socialist developing countries, there are China and Cuba and, among the more market-oriented countries, there are the well-known cases of Sri Lanka, Costa Rica and Kerala, India. In each of these five cases public expenditure has contributed to impressive gains in human development and in none has expenditure on human development resulted in unacceptably slow rates of growth. If there is a conflict between growth and economic security, it must be a very mild one. Probably no such conflict exists.

Some corroboration for these views is provided by a study of a less celebrated case, namely the state of Tamil Nadu, India.[28] In Tamil Nadu, as in India as a whole, protective measures for economic security are available to those who work in the formal sector, i.e. for the government or for large-scale industry. The entitlements include old-age pensions, maternity benefits, injury and invalidity benefits, survivor benefits and a number of health and sickness benefits. In most of India, however, comparable entitlements are not available to the poor, and specifically to those who work in the rural areas or in the informal urban sector. Thus, expenditure on economic security is regressive, favouring those who are relatively better off.

Tamil Nadu is an exception. In addition to the standard programmes for formal sector workers, the state has a history of providing some economic security to the unorganised poor and in 1989 the various entitlement schemes were liberalised and expanded to provide a fairly comprehensive range of benefits. A distinctive feature of Tamil Nadu's programme is that only those identified as 'destitute' are eligible to receive public support. The support for which they are eligible, however, includes an old-age pension (starting at age 65), a pension for the destitute who are physically handicapped (starting at age 45), pensions for destitute widows (age 40) and deserted wives (age 30), maternity assistance for women from poor households, survivor benefits for women (or men) who have lost the primary breadwinner and a marriage grant for girls from poor households.

The benefits are, necessarily, meagre – the old age pension, for example, is Rs 50 per month – and not all eligible recipients in fact receive their entitlements, but a good start has been made and economic security for the most vulnerable groups in the community undoubtedly has increased. The cost in 1989/90 was very modest, only 1.5 per cent of total state expenditure. Thus it certainly is feasible to provide a measure of state-funded economic security to the poorest of the poor. This support, however, should not be seen as standing on its own but rather as supplementing support provided by the family and traditional local institutions and charities.

Based on the experience of Tamil Nadu, it has been estimated that it would be possible to provide a basic minimum package of protective economic security for India as a whole at a cost the country could readily afford.[29] Only those poor persons classified as destitute would be eligible for the five types of benefit included in the basic package, namely, an old-age pension (from age 65), a pension for widows and deserted wives (from age 40), maternity assistance, disability payments (from age 20) and compensation for occupational injuries. This basic package for the very poor need cost no more than 0.3 per cent of gross national product or one per cent of the combined current revenues of the state and central governments.

Tamil Nadu, a major state of India, with a population approaching 50 million, shows what can be done to increase the economic security of those on the margin of survival. What is feasible in Tamil Nadu (and Kerala) surely is feasible in the rest of India. And if economic security is a feasible human development objective in India, one of the poorest countries in the world, then it is equally feasible in all other developing countries. The time has come to put the prevention of severe deprivation, the protection of people's capabilities to lead a minimally acceptable life, high on the list of priorities for public action.

6 Human Development and Sustainable Development

Historical patterns of economic development have produced rapid economic growth in a number of countries for an extended period of time, but these patterns of development also have caused the stock of natural capital in the world to contract considerably and often to become degraded. In addition, there has been a rapid loss of biodiversity. Lastly, there has recently emerged a serious threat of global warming. In the last two decades people have become increasingly aware of the social costs associated with production processes and consumption patterns that harm the environment and this has given rise to demands that henceforth growth should be sustainable.

At the same time, historical patterns of development have been criticised for their failure to put people first and this has led to demands for a change to a human development strategy. There is a danger that human development and sustainable development will be seen as competing strategies, as alternatives between which we must choose. This would be a mistake, for if development is seen as a process that widens people's choices and increases their capabilities, then it must do so not only for the current generation but also for future generations. In this sense, development must be sustainable. Human development thus embraces sustainable development, the latter being particularly concerned with the environmental and inter-generational aspects of human development.

That is, if the objective of human development should properly be seen as the enlargement of human capabilities, as we have argued, then sustainable development can be seen as the permanent enlargement of human capabilities. This is a view which slowly is becoming widely accepted.[1] Sustained development, or a permanent flow of benefits at a given level, requires a constant (or preferably a rising) stock of total capital. The stock of capital consists of natural, physical and human capital, and an implication of this way of viewing development is that sustainability requires that if one component of the total stock of capital is reduced, it must be offset by greater investment in one of the other components. Specifically, sustainable development does not require that the stock of natural capital remain constant, but it does require that there be increases in human and physical capital to compensate for any loss of natural capital.

There are many reasons to believe that this condition for sustainable development has not in the past been met. Both renewable and non-renewable resources have been depleted and, in many countries, there has not been a compensating increase in other forms of capital. The stock of natural capital, in other words, has often been treated as a free good; no provision has been made for depreciation or consumption of the stock of natural capital in national income accounts, and consequently there has been a systematic tendency to overstate the rate of growth.[2] Environmental costs associated with production and consumption processes have largely been ignored and, as a result, levels of income and wellbeing have been exaggerated, as well as rates of growth. It is now recognised that this cannot continue indefinitely.

There are indeed environmental dangers inherent in current rates and patterns of growth in global production and consumption. Yet there is no inherent conflict between development and the environment, between the reduction of poverty and the maintenance of the stocks of natural, physical and human capital at optimal levels, between sustaining biodiversity and increasing the capabilities of people. In so far as the stock of natural capital is damaged or consumed at an excessive rate, the prospects for future development are reduced. In that sense good environmental policies are part of good development policies. This is true whether one is concerned with degradation of the environment at the local level (such as pollution of fresh water supplies), at the international level (such as damage to forests in neighbouring countries downwind of factories emitting sulphur into the air), or at the global level (such as destruction of the ozone layer in the upper atmosphere caused by high emissions of CFCs). Sustained development requires that the basis of life on this planet be preserved and that any depletion of the natural stock of capital be transformed into an equivalent value of human or physical capital. The central point is that if the value of the aggregate stock of capital falls – natural, physical and human – the prospects for development are reduced but, if the value of natural capital falls, development prospects can be maintained provided physical and human capital are increased in compensation.[3]

Damage to the environment is not caused by human activity as such, i.e. consumption, production and reproduction – any more than it is caused by the activities of other species – but by a set of incentives which induces humans to neglect or overlook some of the costs of economic activity, be it production or consumption. All environmental problems – all apparent conflicts between development and the protection of the environment – can be seen as arising ultimately from either (i) government failure, (ii) market failure, (iii) missing markets arising from undefined property rights, or (iv) high discount rates of the poor because of their inability to sustain life without depleting the stock of natural capital.

GOVERNMENT FAILURE AND CLASS BIAS

Government failure in the context of sustainable development refers to actions taken by local, provincial or national governments which create incentives to use the natural stock of capital wastefully and inefficiently. These defective incentives may reflect ignorance on the part of policymakers, but they may also reflect a class bias in policymaking. That is, government intervention may be designed to serve particular economic interests, and policies conventionally described as 'government failure' may be quite successful in their own terms. In what follows, we shall use the phrase 'government failure' in the broadest sense, to cover errors committed out of ignorance, as well as waste and inefficiency knowingly created while favouring the interests of particular classes or groups in society. Examples of government failure in this broad sense include policies which subsidise the cost of water to users, policies which subsidise the cost of land to ranchers and agriculturalists and often encourage otherwise unprofitable economic activities in areas where the resource base is fragile or marginal, and policies which subsidise logging, and provide little incentive for replanting, in the tropical forests of developing countries.

Correction of government failure would automatically reduce the incentive to over-exploit the environment and make investment in physical and human capital relatively more attractive. That is, adoption of a more sustainable path to development would tend to accelerate human development.

Equally important, a greater concern with human development would probably result in more public policy measures to protect the environment and consequently in reduced depletion of the stock of natural capital. The reason for this is partly political. An increase in the human development of the poor – in the form of greater literacy, improved education and increased participation – would 'strengthen their ability to combat environmental degradation of which they are the victims, not perpetrators'.[4] That is, human development could help to counteract the class bias that lies behind much government failure. Some have argued that this 'is potentially the most important linkage between human capital and natural capital' because 'much of the pollution and natural resource depletion in the developing countries, as elsewhere, is driven not by the desperation of the poor, but by the greed and negligence of the rich'.[5] Hence, human development, political participation and environmental protection are closely connected.

A special case of government failure concerns the failure of the standard national income and production accounts to record the depreciation of the value of natural capital. The standard accounts consequently overstate both the rate of growth of the economy and the level of capital formation. In Costa Rica, for example, it is estimated that unrecorded depreciation in the value of the country's forests, soils and fisheries was on average five per cent of GNP per year between 1970 and 1990.[6] In Indonesia, the unrecorded depreciation of its forests, soils and petroleum resources was about 9 per cent of its GDP between 1971 and 1984.[7] These failures to record the consumption of natural capital mean that the official national accounts can be highly misleading, giving a false picture of the level of development.

MARKET FAILURE

The second source of defective incentives arises not from government subsidies and other forms of government failure but from market failure. This was discussed at some length in Chapter 2 in the context of market signals failing to reflect accurately the costs of land use and the benefits of increasing the stock of human capital. In the context of sustainable development, market failure occurs whenever prices generated by the market mechanism fail to reflect fully the costs to the environment and the natural stock of capital of production and consumption activities. In such cases negative externalities ('bads') are produced as well as goods. Where environmental costs are understated by market prices, producers and consumers have an incentive to use resources wastefully and to overproduce those goods that use natural capital intensively.

Unfortunately, many economic processes generate negative externalities and this is particularly true in technologically advanced economies. Examples include the pollution of the air by trucks and automobiles, pollution of rivers and lakes by factories dumping noxious waste in inland waterways, salination of the land in areas where irrigated agriculture unaccompanied by proper drainage is practised, and pollution of coastal waterways by the discharge into the sea of untreated sewage from large cities. Market failure is widespread in the industrialised countries and this accounts for the fact that most global environmental damage is the result of past and current production and consumption patterns in the advanced economies. The industrialised countries, for instance, account for about 75 per cent of the carbon and 90 per cent of the CFC emissions, the two gases believed to cause global warming. In addition, the industrialised countries consume about ten times as much energy, water, minerals and biomass as do the developing countries. Thus the developed countries bear primary responsibility for the present global environmental problems and it is they who have the major obligation to repair the damage. This is a straightforward application of the 'polluter pays' principle.

Note, however, that the existence of negative externalities and market failure do not imply that either developing or developed countries should reduce their rate of growth in the name of sustainable development. If an economic activity produces a negative externality, the activity in question (say, the output of a specific product) should be reduced. Efficiency in resource allocation requires a changed composition of output, not a reduction in aggregate output. The implication of market failure is that governments should intervene to correct market prices so that producers and consumers respond to a set of incentives that accurately reflects all costs, including environmental costs. If this were done, human development activities would become even more attractive than they are now. The general point, however, is that market failure is a cause of defective incentives, not a symptom of excessive growth. The solution is to correct the incentive system, not to restrain the level or rate of growth of net output and income. Indeed, well-conceived environmental policies – sustainable development – would enhance the overall rate of growth, provided the national accounts are improved and growth is measured correctly by taking into account all benefits and all costs of production.

MISSING MARKETS

The third source of defective incentives occurs whenever a market for an environmental service is missing. As explained above in Chapter 2, these so-called missing markets arise when property rights are undefined or unenforced. Examples include unclaimed forest land, common pastures under the control of no particular group or individual, freshwater aquifers from which anyone may extract water by digging a well, and at the global level, the high seas, the upper atmosphere and the polar regions. In cases where property rights are undefined, no one has an incentive to manage the natural asset to ensure a sustained flow of income and everyone with access to the asset has an incentive to extract maximum benefit as quickly as possible. The results are overcutting of forests, overgrazing of pastures, withdrawal of water in excess of the recharge rate, overfishing the oceans, destruction of the upper atmosphere, etc. Here again, however, the solution to the problem of missing markets is to correct the incentive system, by creating enforceable property rights – either individual, collective, state or supranational – not to retard the process of human development or diminish efforts to reduce poverty.

HIGH DISCOUNT RATES

A major cause of environmental problems in developing countries is restricted access by the poor to income-earning opportunities, including opportunities arising from ownership or control of sufficient natural capital to sustain life above a subsistence level. It is becoming widely recognised that in many cases the alleviation of poverty by providing greater access by the poor to resources and employment, and by promoting human development, is probably the most effective policy of sustainable development. A guarantee to the poor of employment, a redistribution of land through a land reform, and a substitution of human capital for natural capital are illustrations of how human development is intimately connected to sustainable development. One can go further, however: human development in some circumstances of acute poverty may be necessary in order to prevent environmental degradation and rapid depletion of the stock of natural capital.

Land degradation and desertification are concentrated in areas where poverty leaves the population with little alternative to the excessive exploitation of resources. Deforestation, too, is often the last resort of people who cannot find other ways to generate a minimum level of income. Overfishing of coastal waters and inland lakes and rivers often occurs because poor fisherfolk have no alternative means of support. That is, because of their very low levels of income, the poor often have high discount rates. Their concern is immediate survival, not maintaining the stock of natural capital so that it can generate a sustained flow of income for the indefinite future. As long as acute poverty persists, the interest of future generations will be ignored and the natural stock of capital will be consumed and damaged. Rural poverty and environmental damage thus often go together, and the solution to the latter is to eliminate the former by adopting a human development strategy.

In conclusion, provided sustainable development is interpreted to mean the preservation of the total and natural stocks of capital at levels which are capable of sustaining indefinitely the human population at current standards of living, there is no conflict between sustainable development and human development. Of course one aspires to more, namely, a substantial reduction in poverty achieved either through a redistribution of income or through growth of average incomes per head. Sustaining the present population at current standards of living is too modest a goal. However, this does not detract from the fact that sustainable development is necessary to permit long-run human development. Equally, human development is essential if the damage currently being inflicted on the environment is to be controlled, and sustainable development is to become a realistic possibility.

7 Finance and Administration

One of the recurring themes of this study is that a decision to adopt a human development strategy does not imply an unusually large state or an unusually heavy burden of taxation. Human development is more concerned about spending priorities than about the total volume of expenditure. How the state spends its money is more important than how much money the state spends. Given that the total resources available to the government in most developing countries is a fifth to a quarter of total income, it should be possible to finance the state's contribution to human development by reallocating expenditure within existing revenue ceilings, without the necessity to raise additional revenues through taxation.

In many countries, however, the extent of reallocation will be quite considerable. Human development is an overall strategy of development, and successful implementation of the strategy does not imply merely adding a few human development activities to the existing array of government spending programmes but, on the contrary, it implies a profound change in public policy and in the composition of state spending. Reallocations are likely to be necessary both within sectors (e.g. health) and between sectors (e.g. reduced spending on fertiliser subsidies and more spending on family planning services). These reallocations, once completed, often will result in a budget with a radically different shape from that found in the majority of developing countries.

There is, of course, no such thing as an ideal or optimal pattern of public expenditure that applies universally, independently of the circumstances of particular countries, and it would be fatuous to suggest otherwise. None the less, it might be useful to draw together the threads of our analysis in previous chapters and present some orders of magnitude so that the reader can visualise the broad contours of the strategy as a whole. This is what is attempted in Table 7.1.

In constructing the 'model budget' in Table 7.1 it is assumed that government revenue is equivalent to 25 per cent of gross national product. This is higher than the average in developing countries but below the ratios that can be found in countries such as Egypt (35.9 per cent), Zimbabwe (35.6 per cent), Tunisia (31.8 per cent), Chile (31.1 per cent), Malaysia (28.9 per cent) and Uruguay (28 per cent). Thus the assumption, while a little optimistic, is not unrealistic. Turning to the expenditure side, we have

103

disaggregated total spending into seven categories, four of which are directly concerned with human development (categories 1–4) and three of which are not (categories 5–7). We have followed the classification of expenditure used by the World Bank except for the guaranteed employment programme (category 4) which we have listed separately.

The allocations within the 'model budget' are presented in two ways; namely, expenditure in each category expressed as a percentage of GNP, and as a percentage of total government expenditure. The actual composition of central government expenditure in Indonesia also is presented so that comparisons can be made between the 'model budget' and the revealed priorities of a large developing country following a more conventional strategy.

Note that in the 'model budget', 66 per cent of government expenditure is allocated to human development activities (categories 1–4), whereas in Indonesia only 11.9 per cent of central government spending is channelled to these areas. Thus if Indonesia were to adopt a human development strategy and were to change its spending priorities to reflect new objectives, the share of expenditure allocated to education, health, social security and employment would have to rise by a multiple of five in order to approximate the priorities embodied in the 'model budget'. The changes contemplated are thus far from marginal.

Table 7.1 Government spending for human development: a model budget

	Percentage of GNP	Percentage of total govt expend. Model	Indonesia
1. Education, training	5.0	20	8.4
2. Health, family planning, etc.	5.0	20	2.0
3. Social security	4.5	18	1.5
food security	(2.0)	(8)	
economic security	(0.5)	(2)	
other, including housing and sanitation	(2.0)	(8)	
4. Guaranteed employment programme	2.0	8	0.0
5. Economic services	3.0	12	27.6
6. Defence, etc.	2.0	8	8.0
7. All other expenditure	3.5	14	52.4
Total	25.0	100	99.9

Within the 'model budget', equal priority is assigned to education, training, research and related activities (category 1) and to public health, nutrition and family planning (category 2), each accounting for about 20 per cent of total expenditure. Social security as a whole (category 3) is allocated 18 per cent of the budget, 8 per cent assigned to food security, 2 per cent to economic security and 8 per cent to all other programmes, including housing, sanitation and clean water. The guaranteed employment scheme (category 4) also is expected to account for about 8 per cent of total government spending. Thus the three major structural reforms discussed in Chapter 5 which require sustained support – guaranteed employment, food security and economic security – absorb only 18 per cent of the budget. (It is assumed that asset redistribution – the other major reform – is a once-for-all measure which does not have recurrent budgetary implications. If it does, e.g. in the form of interest payments on government bonds used to compensate landowners, this would be funded from the allocations in category 7.)

It is envisaged in the 'model budget' that 34 per cent of government expenditure (or 8.5 per cent of GNP) would be devoted to activities not directly connected to human development (categories 5–7). This is a much smaller proportion than one would expect to find in countries following a more conventional strategy of development. Indeed, it is the sharp reduction in resources allocated to categories 5–7 that makes it possible to increase expenditure on human development. It is impossible to be specific about which programmes should be cut or eliminated, but it is clear in general that budgetary savings will largely arise from a combination of (i) a reduction in outlays on defence and related activities, (ii) the elimination of government subsidies to physical inputs, credit and services consumed by upper-income groups, (iii) a sharp reduction and preferably the elimination of deficits in state economic enterprises and (iv) a contraction of expenditure on other government activities of relatively low priority. In addition, we suggest below that human development is consistent with a more streamlined central government bureaucracy. Considerable savings may arise from doing away with the costly and unnecessary administrative machinery established to deliver goods and services to passive beneficiaries. These cuts and savings will not be easy, but they are essential because otherwise it will not be possible to reallocate government spending in favour of human development within a fixed revenue ceiling.

We have assumed so far that government revenues are adequate and, in the 'model budget', we have assumed specifically that total revenues are sufficient to finance an expenditure programme equivalent to 25 per cent of gross national product. In some countries, however, government revenue may not be sufficient to finance a human development strategy and it will consequently be necessary to raise additional funds.

Ignoring the possibility of external financing, there are several options from which to choose. First, the state could raise prices charged for the goods and services it produces for the public. This includes the prices charged by state economic enterprises as well as the charges levied by public utilities for power, water, drainage, telecommunications, etc., when these industries are in the public sector. This possibility was touched upon above in connection with eliminating the deficits of state enterprises, but the general issue is broader than this. In principle, efficiency requires that the price of state-produced goods and services cover long-run marginal costs, including the opportunity cost of capital, and purchasers should expect to have to pay this price. In some cases this implies that state enterprises should behave in a more commercial, profit-oriented way but without abusing their monopoly power. In other cases it may be better to transfer some of the state enterprises to the private sector by direct sale or auction. Provided the goods and services being supplied are consumed directly or indirectly by upper-income groups, there is no conflict between allocative efficiency and distributive equity. However, even when there is a conflict between the two objectives, policymakers should consider whether it would be possible to achieve the distributive objective in some other way, e.g. by increasing expenditure on human development activities oriented toward the poor.

Second, the government could consider imposing or increasing user charges to help recover some of the costs of supplying government services that often are provided free of charge. The main candidates here are health and education services. While we certainly favour the introduction of user charges when this can be done without incurring heavy administrative costs or worsening the distribution of income, we are sceptical of the efficacy of differential rate structures because they tend to become overly elaborate and cumbersome. The objective should be to keep the structure of user fees simple, preferably with a single uniform rate and, where this is desired on grounds of equity, an exemption for members of a well-defined group. User charges are perhaps most effective when the users are predominantly upper-income persons and the costs of supplying the service are high. Examples include tertiary education and services provided by large urban hospitals.

Finally, the government can raise additional revenue by introducing new taxes or increasing the rates (up to a point) of old taxes. Here again, however, one should try to keep the tax system as simple as possible. There are numerous examples of governments in developing countries attempting to use the tax system to achieve multiple objectives, such as redistributing income, promoting investment, encouraging savings, accelerating growth and increasing efficiency. Most of these attempts have been unsuccessful and the country has been encumbered with a tax system that is complex, costly to administer and easy to evade. Experience therefore suggests that the wisest course, even for a human development strategy with a strong redistributive element, is to use the tax system primarily for what it does best, raising revenue. Taxation cannot by itself eliminate poverty or accelerate human development. These objectives are better addressed from the expenditure side of the budget. The role of the tax system is to raise revenue while making certain that the poor are not further impoverished and that human development is not impeded by government taxation.

One of the distinctive features of a human development strategy is that it is not intensive in the use of foreign aid or, indeed, of foreign capital in general. Human development is a strategy that mobilises domestic resources and above all the energy, skills, talents and creativity of a nation's own people. Given that foreign aid and other forms of foreign capital are likely to be less readily available in future than in the past, human development is well suited for those countries which by choice or *faute de mieux* wish to become more self-reliant. Similarly, human development is not a strategy that is intensive in the use of foreign exchange: it does not rely heavily on imported capital and intermediate goods to sustain investment or production. The strategy is likely to be most successful where governments are committed to an open economy, biased neither towards export promotion nor import substitution.

Finally, a human development strategy does rely intensively on certain types of government services and support, above all on services that are in close contact with the grassroots: primary education, village health clinics, guaranteed employment on locally-selected investment projects. This has implications for the administration of development and the empowerment of people. In the final analysis, if human beings are the end of development, if enhancing their capabilities and enlarging their choices is the ultimate objective, then empowerment must be central to what development is all about. Unfortunately the structure of governance in many developing countries – a structure often inherited from the colonial era – is antithetical to empowerment. The reason is that the state apparatus originally was designed to serve the purposes of a colonial administration, maintaining political control over a subject people, exploiting the territory's resources and extracting an economic surplus with the minimum amount of investment. Power was consequently highly centralised. This resulted in efficient administration in its own terms, but the structure of governance was inconsistent with political democracy and participatory development.

Governments in developing countries now have, or should have, new purposes but these new purposes have seldom been reflected in a restructured public administration. There is a strong case in many developing countries for bringing government closer to the people by devolving authority to lower levels of the administration – to provincial, district and local government. There is, however, a paradox here. Where once a highly-centralised administration was an instrument of (colonial) tyranny, today the greater tyranny often is to be found at the local and provincial levels, where large landowners and their allies are able to exercise enormous power. Central government, in comparison, may be relatively benign and farsighted, more inclined to support human development in opposition to the entrenched forces that dominate the countryside. Thus decentralisation is not an unmixed blessing or a goal in itself and it does not necessarily result in empowerment of the people. Decentralisation is most consistent with the goals of human development when it is preceded by measures which redistribute wealth and income in favour of the poor and break the monopoly of power of local vested interests.

Decentralised government is not necessarily cheaper government. Indeed decentralisation in support of human development could well result in a larger civil service and higher expenditure on general administration. The case for decentralisation is not based on smaller government or lower costs but on improvements in the quality of government-supplied services and on increased participation of the population in determining what is to be supplied. The intention, certainly, is to get a heavy-handed central government 'off the backs of the people', not in order to reduce costs while leaving the people to fend for themselves, but in order to provide the essential public services needed to accelerate human development and increase the wellbeing of the people.

PUBLIC SECTOR PRICES, CHARGES AND COSTS

The public sector in many developing countries is quite large and supplies a wide range of goods and services from luxury international airline travel to nitrogenous fertiliser. The state enterprises that produce these goods and services often have to be subsidised because their receipts from sales fail to cover their total costs. Some of these subsidies, as discussed in Chapter 3, can be justified on efficiency grounds, because social costs and benefits differ from costs and benefits as measured by the market. Subsidies to state enterprises with important training, education or scientific research functions might fall under this category. In other cases the subsidies could perhaps be justified on grounds of equity, as a way of improving the distribution of income; but subsidies to state enterprises will almost always be a second-best way to achieve distributive objectives. The remaining subsidies, however, which account for most of the losses, can be justified neither on grounds of market failure nor on grounds of equity. State enterprises which incur such losses should be required to reduce their costs or raise prices or else they should be shut down or sold off.

Increasing the price of goods and services supplied by state enterprises can reduce claims on the exchequer to finance enterprise deficits and release funds for activities directly connected with human development. Similarly the government can impose user charges or fees for the services it provides. User charges, however, are likely to be appropriate only for certain types of services. In some cases, e.g. parks, beaches and other recreational facilities, nominal fees may be all that is required to prevent excessive use of the facilities and cover most of the day-to-day running costs. In the case of other natural resources which constitute part of the natural capital of a country, the issues are rather different, e.g. the optimal rate of exploiting fishery or timber resources, or the optimal rate of depleting petroleum, gas and other mineral deposits. Questions of conservation and the transformation of natural capital into physical and human capital come into play here. Some of the relevant principles were touched upon in Chapter 1.

The case for user charges for government-produced services, as opposed to charges for the use of government-owned natural assets, is similar to the case for full pricing of products produced by state enterprises. The qualifications – externalities and equity – also are similar. Equity considerations suggest that user charges are highly appropriate for public services which benefit mainly middle- and upper-income groups. Tertiary education is a prime example, and it is noteworthy that in South Korea user charges in higher education cover about 46 per cent of operating costs. The case for user charges for primary and secondary education is weak, although in China even the poor must make a token payment towards the cost of primary education and basic health services. Considerations of equity may tempt policymakers to introduce differential user charges for health and education based on the ability to pay. Such systems normally should be avoided: they are administratively costly and cumbersome and often fail to affect the target groups in the way intended.

Apart from increasing prices and imposing user charges, governments should attempt to lower costs of public sector activities. A human development strategy, by its very nature – people-centred, participatory, democratic

– is well suited to low-cost methods of production and supply. The administration of primary schools and health clinics, for example, can be delegated to the local level, i.e. to the villages, small towns, communities and neighbourhoods where the facilities are located. Decentralisation as such does not guarantee that costs will be lower – and in fact the advantages of economies of scale can sometimes be lost – but it does create a possibility for mobilising locally-available low-cost resources, increasing the influence of intended beneficiaries, giving them a voice in what services are most needed and how they can best be supplied, and hence increasing the likelihood that the quality of the public services will improve. In this sense decentralisation can be very cost-effective.

Participation is, of course, an end in itself; it is also a way of enhancing people's capabilities. Participation and its corollary, empowerment, enable people to exercise more control over their own lives. In allowing people to exercise control, governments help to unleash their energies, their commitment, their productivity and creativity. At the local level where people are most able to manage their own affairs, democracy clearly can help to enhance efficiency. In such a context, for example, teachers are more likely to become part of the community instead of representatives of an outside administration. Local people are more likely to be willing to supplement the salaries of teachers (possibly with payments in kind), to pay for some school supplies or to donate their own labour and materials to build and maintain a school. In such a context people cease to be objects of development and become the instruments of their own development, donating their time, energy and funds because they, their families and their friends will benefit directly.

In some cases the physical facilities, where they exist, can be used more intensively. For example, double shifts may be used in schools, thereby reducing the cost per student of physical capital. In other cases, less-qualified workers, quickly trained, can be substituted for highly-qualified workers whose training is lengthy and costly. The so-called barefoot doctors in China are an early example of how health workers with few formal medical qualifications can be used to extend the coverage and the effectiveness of an entire health care system. Teaching assistants or helpers can play the same role in primary schools. These are illustrations of how the costs of public services can be reduced.

TAXATION AND HUMAN DEVELOPMENT

Let us turn now to a discussion of two points: how taxation can be used to raise additional revenues when existing resources are inadequate and how the tax system should be reformed if it acts as an obstacle to human development. Governments usually have greater control over the allocation of expenditure than over the ways expenditure is financed. In particular, governments in developing countries have found it difficult to tax people in accordance with their ability to pay. Upper-income groups have been able to use their power and influence to get governments to subsidise activities of interest to themselves while at the same time ensuring that they are taxed relatively lightly. Thus both the income and expenditure sides of the state budget tend to favour the rich. The tax system often is regressive and upper-income groups are able to escape paying their share by taking advantage of tax exemptions, income deductions and tax credits included in the revenue code as well as, of course, by outright tax-evasion. It has turned out to be especially difficult to tax capital, in part because the valuation of capital assets such as land is difficult and in part because of the international mobility of financial capital.

Few tax systems in developing countries have succeeded in bringing about a significant redistribution of income by imposing a heavy tax burden on the rich. The richest five or ten per cent of the population almost always manage to avoid paying a large portion of the taxes for which they would appear to be liable. As a result, the post-tax distribution of income has a tendency to reflect the underlying distribution of wealth. Hence one reason for our emphasis on asset-redistribution in Chapter 5. Some progressivity can be achieved, however, by exempting the lowest income groups from the payment of some taxes, notably income taxes. Given the administrative and political difficulties of using the tax system for redistributive purposes, a government pursuing a human development strategy probably would be well-advised to concentrate on the distribution of the benefits from public expenditure and use the tax system to ensure that adequate revenues are available to finance planned expenditures.

(i) Import Duties and Export Taxes

The base of a tax system can be almost anything – wealth, income, consumption, domestic or foreign trade – but many developing countries place heavy reliance on import duties and export taxes. The proportion may have fallen in the last decade or so, but many developing countries still obtain between a quarter and a third of their government revenue from taxes on international trade. Heavy taxation of internationally-traded commodities – by increasing the cost of exporting and shielding import-substituting industries from competition – tends to weaken the competitiveness of developing countries and makes their fiscal position vulnerable to fluctuations and instability originating abroad.

In Indonesia in the late 1970s and early 1980s, for example, two-thirds of tax revenue came from taxes on the export of oil and liquefied natural gas. Had it not implemented a major tax reform before international oil prices fell sharply in the late 1980s, Indonesia would have encountered a fiscal crisis and been forced either to cut government expenditure sharply or tolerate huge fiscal deficits.[1] Similarly, two-thirds of Venezuela's public expenditure is financed by taxing exports of petroleum but unlike Indonesia, Venezuela did not introduce a tax reform and consequently the country ran into severe revenue problems when oil prices fell. A combination of low oil prices and depleted oil reserves does not augur well for the fiscal future of the country.[2]

Other countries are highly dependent on revenues from import tariffs. The situation could be improved – revenue stability increased and international competitiveness enhanced – if governments were to shift the tax base toward domestic sources of revenue while maintaining low, uniform tariff rates on imports and exports.

(ii) Income Taxes

In principle, income taxes, and in particular taxes on personal incomes, should be attractive to governments which have adopted a human development strategy. In practice, however, personal income tax systems usually have not worked well in developing countries. Income taxes are attractive, first, because they can be made to be progressive and, second, because, if progressive, revenues rise faster than national income, thereby imparting a degree of elasticity to the entire tax system. Progressive personal income tax systems, however, work best in countries where price inflation is low or moderate, the economy is fully monetised and accurate business records are kept, administration is honest and technically competent, literacy is universal, capital is immobile across international borders and tax compliance is voluntary. These conditions are rarely found in developing countries and, as a result, the revenue yield of income taxes has tended to be low. Income taxes are much more difficult to administer than indirect taxes on consumption, and in those developing countries which have personal income taxes, seldom more than five per cent of the population is covered, primarily salaried persons working in the urban formal sector.[3]

Income from property (retained profits, dividends, interest, rent) frequently is taxed at very low rates if at all. The tax system thus has a bias in favour of investments in physical capital (the income from which escapes taxation) and against human capital (the income from which, if sufficiently high, may be liable to income taxation). Erosion of the income-tax base because of avoidance and evasion is common and severe, especially in the case of income from property. In Jamaica, for instance, it is estimated that because of inability to enforce tax legislation fully, actual revenues are only 54.4 per cent of potential revenues. If, to the loss of revenue due to non-reporting of income, one adds revenue lost because of loopholes in the tax code, then actual revenue falls to 38.2 per cent of potential revenue.[4] It is the self-employed who are in the best position to evade taxation, and the incidence of evasion tends to increase with the level of income. As a result, a notionally progressive income tax system in fact is transformed into a regressive tax system.

Personal income taxes in developing countries thus tend to discriminate against income from human capital and to be inequitable. Income from physical and financial capital escapes most taxation. Income from labour, in contrast, is taxed relatively heavily, particularly when one takes into account the fact that the cost of accumulating human capital – the costs of education and training – are not allowed to be deducted from taxable income.

Taxes on corporate incomes and profits are easier to administer than taxes on personal incomes and, in principle, it should be possible to raise large revenues from a relatively small number of corporate taxpayers, domestic and foreign. However, governments must beware of imposing very high average or marginal tax rates lest the after-tax rate of return on assets be pushed below what can be obtained abroad. This would almost certainly precipitate capital flight. The mobility of capital, in other words, imposes a limit on the extent to which taxation can be used for redistributive purposes. It is partly for this reason that the income tax system in most developing countries taxes physical and financial capital rather lightly compared to human capital. This introduces a bias against labour and human capital relative to other factors of production.

(iii) Taxes on Wealth

Many of the problems that arise in taxing income also arise when taxing wealth. Since wealth and political power often go together, wealthy taxpayers in developing countries often succeed in shifting the tax burden from wealth to consumers or workers. The least difficult wealth taxes to collect are those on highly visible and immovable assets such as urban real estate and agricultural land. Taxes on urban property are sometimes said to be regressive, but this is unlikely to be true in most developing countries. In fact, property taxes are likely to be a more progressive way to cover the cost of providing urban services than progressively differentiated user charges. The reason for this is that the income elasticity of demand for housing (and other urban property) is greater than the elasticity of demand for the services themselves and hence spending on housing rises proportionately faster, as incomes increase, than spending on urban utilities and other services. The problem for the tax authorities is how to obtain and maintain accurate estimates of the value of urban property. Inevitably there is a conflict, on the one hand, between accuracy and fairness and, on the other, the administrative costs of valuation and tax collection. Once again, our advice is to keep it simple and use rough methods of valuation in order to keep administrative costs low.

Turning to the rural sector, the greatest difficulty policymakers confront in taxing agricultural land is undoubtedly political: the power of the land-owning class. Where land is distributed highly unequally – a common phenomenon – the best solution, as argued in Chapter 5, is land reform. If land taxation were to accompany land redistribution, as we recommend, an equitable agricultural tax system could readily be established. Such a system, moreover, would be very broadly based and would provide revenue that could be collected at low cost.

Where land reform is impossible, it still is worthwhile introducing a land tax, provided of course that it is politically feasible. Even a very simple land tax can contribute significantly to government revenues while also being equitable. The key to land taxation is to base it on information that is readily available or that can be obtained at low cost. The revenue authorities need to know only four facts in order to design an effective system of agricultural land taxation: the area of the property, its location, its soil quality classification and the name of the owner.[5] In some countries the most difficult piece of information to obtain might appear to be soil quality, but recent developments in satellite imaging have made it much easier to estimate the potential fertility of the soil. In practice it may be more difficult to discover the name of the owner!

The easiest land tax to administer is one with a flat rate per unit of land with an exemption for holdings below a threshold size. If it is desired to have a progressive scale, then several rates per unit of land will have to be introduced, with the rates rising with the total area of the property. This can quickly become complex to administer – particularly when landowners have several properties in different regions with different soil qualities –

and we suggest that the fewer the number of tax rates, the better. Exemption of small holdings from taxation can go a long way toward making the system of land taxation moderately progressive. Exemption also ensures that the poor are not further impoverished by taxation. In Indonesia, for example, the property tax reforms of the 1980s included an exemption of US $1600 for all buildings, rural and urban, and the effect of this was to exclude from taxation virtually all houses in the rural areas and most houses occupied by low-income families in the urban areas.[6]

(iv) Indirect Taxes

During the last 10 to 15 years, indirect taxes on consumption have become the principal means of raising revenue. Indeed, in the 1980s, indirect taxes accounted for more than half of government revenue in two-thirds of the developing countries. Value added tax in particular has been prominent in many of the most recent tax reforms and has been successful in raising revenue. The main concern about value added tax and other forms of indirect taxation is their effects on the post-tax distribution of income. Indirect taxation tends to be regressive.

The poor in developing countries, while usually not subject to income and wealth taxes, do nevertheless pay a significant amount of taxes. The urban poor, for instance, pay taxes equivalent to about 10 per cent of their income and much of this is accounted for by indirect taxes. A study of the Jamaican tax system revealed that the taxes which had the greatest impact on the poor were taxes levied on food and taxes on intermediate and capital goods used to produce food. Exemption of a few basic items such as cornmeal and condensed milk from the value added tax could go some way toward reducing the tax burden on low-income households.[7] Thus it is possible to combine the efficiency of indirect taxes in raising revenue with measures to temper their regressive effects. Exemption from taxation of basic foods consumed largely by the poor would be consistent with human development and its goal of nutritional adequacy; it would also be desirable on grounds of distributive justice.

Excise taxes, such as those on beer, spirits and tobacco, pose interesting problems for a tax system concerned with poverty and human development. Excise taxes are very good for generating revenue because of the low price elasticity of demand of the goods taxed, but this low price elasticity tends to result in a regressive impact of the taxes on the incomes of the poor, who buy large quantities of the taxed items. It is sometimes argued that high excise taxes on beer, spirits and tobacco reduce the ability of the poor to purchase basic necessities, including nutritious food. Against this is the argument that consumption of beer, spirits and tobacco produces large negative externalities (violence, death, accidents, illness) and the poor are no more entitled than the rich to inflict these heavy costs on the rest of society, including other members of the consumer's household.[8] Moreover, immoderate consumption of these items has the unfortunate effect of markedly depreciating the stock of human capital, reducing longevity, productivity and capabilities, and hence high excise taxes are not inconsistent with a human development strategy.

(v) Tax Administration

There are many examples in developing countries of taxes with considerable revenue potential failing to deliver as expected simply because of weak tax administration. Part of the problem is technical: the taxes are too complex to administer or too difficult and costly to collect. Tax simplification often goes hand-in-hand with good tax administration. An obvious way to simplify a tax system is to eliminate many of the deductions, exemptions and credits that tend to become imbedded in the tax structure with the passage of time. If there are to be exemptions, the beneficiaries should be the poor rather than the rich. Yet unfortunately it commonly is the other way round.

Tax simplification can also be achieved by not incorporating non-revenue objectives into the tax system. Tax preferences given to favoured economic activities reduce total revenues while making the tax system more complex. They often conflict with one another or have effects which are incidental to or contradictory with the original objectives. Again, the rich invariably are in the best position to lobby for and benefit from preferential treatment. Governments which have adopted a human development strategy may be tempted to use the tax system to encourage human capital formation, e.g. by allowing deductions for the cost of training or formal education, but this objective probably can be better promoted by expenditure policies rather than tax policy. Tax gimmicks seldom are successful.

Ultimately the main reason that tax administration is often weak and ineffective is political. Just as upper-income groups are able to ensure that they receive a disproportionate share of government subsidies, so too they are able to ensure that they escape much of the burden of taxation. This pattern of subsidy and taxation occurs not by accident but by design. Experience has shown, however, that this inequity is easier to remedy by changing the composition of government expenditure than by changing the structure of the tax system. Governments wishing to promote human development are therefore well advised to concentrate their attention on the expenditure side of the budget, not only because human development objectives can be achieved this way with less difficulty but also because politically it may be unwise to fight a battle on two fronts simultaneously. The first priority should be to assemble a powerful political coalition to support a human development strategy on the basis of benefits arising from changes in government expenditure. Once this has been achieved, it should be possible to address the inequities imbedded in the tax system and by correcting these to bring about further improvements in the distribution of income and wealth. Governments which enjoy broad popular support are in the best position successfully to implement progressive tax reforms.

FOREIGN AID

During the last 45 years many developing countries have come to depend on external funds to finance their development programmes. Most of this external capital has consisted of some form of foreign aid – untied grants, bilateral tied grants and loans, surplus food products sold for local currency, multilateral loans provided at a subsidised interest rate, technical assistance – although in the 1970s loans from international commercial banks were significant and in a small number of countries direct private foreign investment has played a role. The results of foreign aid programmes, whether bilateral or multilateral, have in general been disappointing: they have done little to promote growth and even less to promote human development.[9]

The rationale for foreign aid is that it is essential to compensate for an assumed shortage of domestic finance in developing countries. That is, foreign capital (in the form of foreign aid) supplements inadequate domestic savings and permits a country to have a higher rate of investment than would otherwise be possible. Greater investment, in turn, leads to faster growth. This chain of reasoning, however, is based on a false assumption: namely, that the chief obstacle in developing countries is a deficiency of physical capital and modern technology. The contrary view, the one that we support, is that the principal obstacle to vigorous, sustainable growth in developing countries is the inadequacy of human development. Foreign aid has not in general been aimed at human development nor has it in practice encouraged human development indirectly. Inflows of foreign capital have tended to reproduce and reinforce the misallocations of domestic public expenditure that have been such a prominent feature of most government budgets.

Even if one believes, contrary to the accumulating evidence, that the engine of growth consists solely or primarily of investment in physical capital, it does not follow that developing countries are incapable of generating sufficient savings to finance that investment. Again, the evidence is clear that developing countries do have the capacity to attain high rates of savings and many have in fact done so. In 1990, for example, gross domestic savings in countries classified by the World Bank as low-income economies were 28 per cent of gross domestic product whereas the savings rate in the high-income economies (including the OECD countries) was much lower than this, at 22 per cent.[10] The problem in developing countries has not been an inability to generate savings for capital formation but to retain their capital domestically and prevent it from leaking abroad. There is a tendency in developing countries for capital to emigrate to more developed countries where it can obtain a higher rate of return. This tendency applies both to finance capital (liquid savings) as well as to human capital in the form of managerial, professional and technical personnel and of highly-skilled and educated workers.[11]

The meagre flows of foreign aid received by developing countries have sometimes had perverse effects, reducing the domestic rate of savings and encouraging capital flight by lowering the real rate of interest and temporarily appreciating the exchange rate. Hence foreign aid has contributed to the problem it was intended to correct.[12] Aid has been concentrated on a small number of countries. It has often been used to finance military expenditure, to enlarge the bureaucracy or to reduce the need for increased taxation. Where aid has resulted in increased investment in physical capital, it has typically financed large, capital-intensive projects with relatively low rates of return. Where it has been directed at human development activities, concentration usually has been on the top of the expenditure pyramid, e.g. financing highly-visible and expensive university facilities and urban hospitals. The social rates of return on these projects have been relatively low and the benefits have largely bypassed the poor.

Thus foreign aid is neither necessary in theory for a human development strategy nor has it been effective in practice. One can, of course, always hope that aid policies will be reformed and aid flows increased, but history provides little basis for such hopes. Human development, in contrast, permits a more self-reliant pattern of development. It is a strategy that mobilises local resources, that concentrates on enlarging the latent capabilities of all people and that can be financed domestically without the need to depend on external subventions or charity. Indeed, one of the attractive features of a human development strategy, for those governments which seek it, is that it liberates a country from dependence on foreign aid.

DECENTRALISATION AND EMPOWERMENT

It goes without saying that a human development strategy cannot be implemented if the revenues available to the government from domestic and foreign sources are inadequate. In addition, human development requires a public administration that is well adapted to the strategy and capable of implementing the tasks for which it is responsible. Throughout this essay we have touched on several issues concerning the structure and role of state institutions in a human development strategy: the overall size of the state, the degree of decentralisation and its relationship to participation and empowerment, the administration of tax reforms, etc. We now pull together the threads of our analysis and examine public administration in the round.

Our central conclusion is that while the volume of work would be no higher, the intellectual demands placed on administrative capacities by human development will be greater than under more conventional strategies. The public administration will be asked to perform more complex tasks (e.g. to devise a calculus of benefits and costs of human development expenditure) and to relate to the public in a different way. The system of public administration consistent with a human development strategy is substantially different from that currently found in most developing countries. The strategy is not primarily concerned with social welfare intervention – the delivery of entitlements to passive beneficiaries – but with the empowerment of people and the liberation of their productive initiatives and creativity so that they can provide for themselves. Human development is about freedom and responsibility, liberation and self-help.

This is the context in which the role of the state should be seen. It is common these days for the state to be viewed as a source of inefficiency and a bureaucratic obstacle to development. This view is a reaction to an earlier one in which a highly centralised state was advocated with responsibilities for central planning and the direct management of major industries. The pendulum has now swung to the opposite extreme: wholesale privatisation of state enterprises and a decentralised administrative structure are advocated. Supporters of human development have also argued in favour of decentralisation, but their objective is fundamentally different from those who wish to construct a nightwatchman state with minimal powers and responsibilities.

As has been shown in this essay, human development requires an activist state, but an activist state which is able to enlist and mobilise people to promote their own development. The corollary of this is slightly paradoxical: in so far as the state pursues this objective successfully, it tends progressively to relieve itself of its traditional functions. The need for continuous intervention diminishes and with it the maze of bureaus required for monitoring, supervision and control that is such a prominent characteristic of state activity in most developing countries. In the long-run, a human development strategy implies a gradual but decided reduction in the role of the state.

This will not occur because human development is best left to the unrestricted operation of market forces. Indeed, market processes on their own are not capable of generating correct signals, of producing an efficient structure of incentives, if for no other reason than the web of positive externalities, complementarities and linkages associated with human development expenditures. No, the role of the state should gradually diminish because human development is best left to human beings themselves, as the direct participants in expanding their own capabilities. Some of the functions of the state gradually will be replaced by the institutions of civil society. In the short run, however, the objective of human development can be served either by a centralised administration or a highly decentralised public administration, depending on the configuration of economic and political power in the country concerned.

Decentralisation of the state should not be confused with empowerment of people. Depending on the circumstances, decentralisation and empowerment can be in conflict, and in many cases they actually have been. It is perhaps useful to distinguish between administrative and political decentralisation.[13] Most efforts to decentralise in developing countries have been administrative in character. That is, the primary purpose has been to increase the efficiency of government operations, not to enhance the political power of people. Political decentralisation, in contrast, is not concerned primarily with increasing efficiency – improving the delivery mechanism of government services, removing bottlenecks and reducing delays, increasing the ability to recover costs – but with the devolution of power to the grassroots. Empowerment may result in greater efficiency, e.g. by mobilising people in support of government initiatives and programmes, but that is not its purpose. Empowerment is an end in itself and should be judged in those terms and not in terms of its functional relationship to other worthy objectives such as cost-effectiveness or efficiency.

Decentralisation cannot be divorced from the political context in which it occurs. If the people do not exercise democratic control over the central apparatus of the state, it is unlikely that decentralisation of the state will be accompanied by increased political power of the people. If the political structure is undemocratic and authoritarian, administrative decentralisation is likely either to maintain or even reinforce central authority. In the late colonial period, for instance, decentralisation sometimes was used as a device to enlist the cooperation of local leaders and broaden the base of support for colonial rule. Similarly in South Africa, under pressure to become more democratic and less authoritarian, the apartheid state responded in the 1980s by introducing a programme of regional and urban decentralisation. While ostensibly democratic, the real intent of the administrative reforms was to increase the power of the centre over local government, depoliticise the black population and produce a new group of political collaborators.[14] Those who opposed apartheid and aspired to a democratic society resisted administrative decentralisation and concentrated their efforts on gaining control of the central state apparatus itself.

Consider a less extreme case, that of Nepal. Decentralisation within this country of 18.9 million persons frequently has been recommended both by outside consultants and officials within the government. One reason for the recommendation is the many inefficiencies that arise from attempting to administer a very backward economy through a highly centralised political authority. Yet the experience of Nepal illustrates why administrative decentralisation is doomed to failure in the absence of a devolution of political power.

Nepal is highly stratified, economically, socially and politically. About 90 per cent of the labour force is engaged in agriculture and lives in rural areas. The ownership of land, however, is highly concentrated and the top 3 per cent of landowners possess nearly 40 per cent of the land. As a result, the distribution of income in Nepal is one of the most unequal in Asia. Decentralisation in Nepal has historically been supported by two groups: populist opponents of the regime and modernist administrators in government. The populists supported decentralisation because they believed it would result in a reduction in the power of the central bureaucracy in the capital and encourage grassroots development. The modernising administrators supported decentralisation as a way to respond to pressure for more local participation without having to legalise opposition political parties. That is, administrative decentralisation was viewed as a tactic to defuse demands for more radical social and political change.

Not surprisingly, decentralisation in Nepal has done little to encourage popular democracy. Villages and districts have little voice and exercise little influence over national policies. Such grassroots participation as exists is controlled and manipulated by the rural elite and local government officials. At the village and ward levels the political system is dominated by rich farmers.[15] If the distribution of wealth and income at the local level are highly unequal and political authority is highly concentrated, as in Nepal, administrative decentralisation is unlikely to result in political decentralisation and the empowerment of the population. Conservative landed elites usually dominate local politics in agrarian societies. The outcome of a policy of decentralisation in such societies normally is doubly disadvantageous: namely, very little actual administrative decentralisation, plus the capture by large landowners of whatever political decentralisation occurs. Compared to this, a centralised administration may be preferable.

In the final analysis human development cannot be separated from participatory development. The goal of human development is to help people realise their own potential, to develop their intellectual, technical and organisational capabilities. Thus human development inescapably is development *by* the people if it is to be development *for* the people.[16] In order to fulfil their potential, people must participate actively in constructing their own autonomous, democratic organisations – including, of course, their political organisations. Political empowerment is an integral aspect of participatory development. Those from outside the community – whether representatives of government or non-governmental organisations – who help people construct their grassroots institutions can be most effective when they function chiefly as facilitators, catalysts or animators. An activist state can encourage or animate human development but it cannot engineer it. That must be done by the people themselves and experience suggests that direct democracy at the local level is the best way to foster it. The role of catalyst or animator, depending on the configuration of political power, can be played either by the institutions of local government or by a centralised state operating through mass mobilisation campaigns, i.e. mass literacy campaigns, mass immunisation campaigns, mass rural construction campaigns and the like. It would be wrong to assume that local bureaucracies are more sympathetic to grassroots democracy than are centralised bureaucracies. Experience suggests, however, that a programme of decentralisation is most successful when local government works in concert with active institutions of civil society, such as community organisations, trade unions and peasant associations.

The connections at the local level between direct democracy and human development are fairly clear. Difficulties arise when large-scale projects are considered and the geographical area encompasses a number of communities or villages. The administration of secondary schools or regional hospitals is an example of what we have in mind. Once one moves beyond the local level, more complex institutions become necessary and direct democracy inevitably has to give way to representative democracy. That is, once one moves beyond the local level, it becomes necessary to delegate authority to leaders who are entrusted to safeguard and advance the interests of a fairly large group. Decision-making inevitably becomes more centralised, but this need not be in conflict with direct democracy at the community level. Indeed, the centralisation necessary for the minimal coordination of governmental activities should be used to facilitate local democracy.

While the historical evolution of national institutions and the concrete political and economic realities of countries will differ, the model which would appear to be most supportive of a human development strategy is one which promotes democracy 'from the bottom up' rather than 'from the top down'. This is because a human development strategy places special emphasis on small, widely dispersed, labour-intensive investment activities such as primary schools, community health clinics, micro-irrigation schemes and local sanitation systems. Since it is at this grassroots level that direct democracy is most likely to flourish, it makes sense on both economic and political grounds for a state committed to human development to direct its efforts toward strengthening the basic organs of self-government in the rural villages and urban neighbourhoods. The local institutions of civil society, in conjunction with local government organisations, can function as 'schools of democracy' in which people acquire experience in taking control of their own lives, individually and collectively. Once the foundation is secure, other floors in the edifice of democracy can be constructed at ever-higher levels.

The opposite approach is to try to promote democracy 'from the top down'. This approach has become widespread in developing countries in recent years and the experience of Bangladesh is illustrative of the consequences. The central government has decentralised some decision-making and revenue-generating functions to intermediate regional levels; namely, to districts and sub-districts, but it has not increased the responsibilities and authority of the basic unit of local government, the union council, although it has a long history. Local government, in other words, continues to be of marginal significance even after decentralisation. Grassroots organisations have in the past filled part of the void and have taken responsibility for the maintenance of local roads, small irrigation systems, primary schools, local water supply and village health and nutrition services. Rather than build on these embryonic institutions and use them to promote human development, the central government has ignored and neglected them and in many instances allowed them to die. Despite this unfortunate history, new NGOs have emerged and in some cases have achieved considerable success. The best-known examples are the Bangladesh Rural Advancement Committee, the Grameen Bank and Proshika. Evidently the tradition of local, self-help organisations has not disappeared completely and with support from government, local institutions could perhaps be revived and used to accelerate human development.[17]

The central government in Bangladesh has tended to distance itself from the non-governmental organisations whereas it should instead regard the efforts of NGOs as complementary to its own. With a little encouragement, it is likely that NGOs could provide even more assistance to grassroots organisations than they do at present. As it is, 55 per cent of the total budget of NGOs in Bangladesh is allocated to human development activities. A vigorous civil society consisting of independent organisations such as NGOs, trade unions, farmers associations, women's associations and youth organisations can contribute much to a broadly-based programme in support of human development. In Bangladesh, however, the success of the NGOs in advancing human development merely underlines the government's own lack of initiative. As far as human development is concerned, decentralisation in Bangladesh has been a red herring.

It is often claimed that administrative decentralisation results in a more efficient delivery of public services than is possible under a centralised system. This claim should, however, be regarded with scepticism. Decentralisation in practice often consists of little more than an enlargement and extension of the government's bureaucracy, a multiplication of posts and offices at lower levels of administration. Problems of coordination and communication often become worse: delays increase, costs mount. Decentralisation is associated not with streamlined administration but with a proliferation of bureaucracy. There is thus a danger that decentralisation will promote neither democracy nor efficiency. Empowerment, on the other hand, is not only democratic, but may also be efficient. It calls for a streamlined central administration which devolves authority as much as possible to the local level. By enlisting the active participation of the people instead of relying on a cumbersome bureaucracy to 'deliver' services to beneficiaries who have little voice in what is delivered and how it is delivered, empowerment may actually be more cost-effective than the alternatives. The experience of West Bengal, India suggests that this may have happened there.[18] Where this does occur, empowerment, human development and economic efficiency are inextricably intertwined. They are the principal components of a strategy that puts people first.

Appendix: The Human Development Index

The Human Development Index (HDI) represents an attempt to move away from a production-oriented view of development (centred on GDP or GNP) towards a people-oriented view of development. The HDI, however, is not an alternative to GDP as an index: the two indicators measure different things. Gross domestic product is a measure of material output of goods and services, whereas the HDI is a measure of human progress, viewed in an international comparative context. The Human Development Index uses three components as proxies for human progress; namely,

(i)   longevity, measured by life expectancy at birth;
(ii) knowledge, measured by the adult literacy rate and mean years of schooling;
(iii) income, which is assumed to exhibit diminishing returns in terms of the amount needed for a decent standard of living.

The international comparative dimension is introduced when each of the three components of the HDI is expressed as an index. The index of longevity (I_l) is defined as

$$\frac{L_{max} - L_c}{L_{max} - L_{min}}, \text{ where}$$

L_{max} = the highest life expectancy observed in the sample of countries being considered;
L_{min} = the lowest life expectancy observed in the sample of countries being considered;
L_c = life expectancy in the country in question.

The index of knowledge (I_k) is defined as

$$W_1 \left[\frac{R_{max} - R_c}{R_{max} - R_{min}} \right] + W_2 \left[\frac{S_{max} - S_c}{S_{max} - S_{min}} \right], \text{ where}$$

R_{max} = the highest adult literacy rate observed in the sample of countries being observed (and *mutatis mutandis* for R_{min} and R_c);
S_{max} = the highest mean years of schooling observed in the sample of countries being observed (and *mutatis mutandis* for S_{min} and S_c);
W_1 = a weight of 2/3 for literacy and
W_2 = a weight of 1/3 for schooling.

The index of income (I_y) is slightly more complicated. It is assumed that the contribution of income to human development diminishes as per capita income (y) rises. Following Atkinson, the wellbeing derived from income (W_y) is assumed to take the following form:

$$W_{(y)} = \frac{1}{1 - \epsilon} \times y^{1-\epsilon}$$

The parameter ϵ measures the extent of diminishing returns. If $\epsilon = 0$ there are no diminishing returns; as ϵ approaches 1, the equation becomes $W_{(y)} = \log y$.

For the purposes of the HDI, ϵ is set equal to zero in all countries whose per capita income (y) is less than y*, the average official poverty-line income in nine industrial countries (Australia, Canada, Germany, the Netherlands, Norway, Sweden, Switzerland, the UK and the USA). Where y < y*, countries are considered to be poor and there are no diminishing returns to income. For incomes between y* and 2y*, ϵ is set equal to 1/2. For incomes between 2y* and 3y*, ϵ is set equal to 2/3, and so on. The weights are arbitrary but they do capture the idea of a diminishing contribution of income to human development. In every case income is defined as real GDP per capita, i.e. GDP measured in terms of purchasing power parity, and it is this which is adjusted by the relevant ϵ.

The index of income (I_y) then becomes

$$\frac{Y_{max} - Y_c}{Y_{max} - Y_{min}}, \text{ where}$$

Y_{max} = the highest adjusted (for diminishing returns) real (purchasing power parity) gross domestic product per capita observed in the sample of countries being considered (and *mutatis mutandis* for Y_{min} and Y_c).

The three component indexes are then added together and divided by three to obtain an overall index of deprivation (I):

$$I = (I_l + I_k + I_y)/3.$$

Note that in computing I, the indexes for longevity, knowledge and income are given equal (arbitrary) weights. The Human Development Index for a country is then simply 1 − I. That is

$$HDI_c = 1 - I_c.$$

ADJUSTING FOR THE DISTRIBUTION OF INCOME

It is possible to adjust any of the component indexes of the HDI to take inequality into account. In practice, so far only the index of income (I_y) has been adjusted. This is done by multiplying I_y by (1 − G), where G is the Gini coefficient of the distribution of income. The Human Development Index for a country then becomes

$$HDI_c = 1 - \frac{\left[I_l + I_k + I_y(1 - G)\right]}{3}.$$

Income-distribution-adjusted HDIs have been calculated for 53 countries. In

Table A1.1 we compare the HDI values (and ranks) with the income-distribution-adjusted HDI values (and ranks) for these 53 countries. The HDI refers to 1990 although the Gini coefficients (which do not change much from one year to another) refer to various years between 1975 and 1988. The countries are listed in order of their income-distribution-adjusted HDI. It can be seen at a glance that adjusting income for inequality does indeed alter the ranking of countries.

Table A1.1   HDI and income-distribution-adjusted HDI compared

Country	HDI rank	HDI value	Income-distribution-adjusted HDI rank	value
Japan	2	0.981	1	0.979
Netherlands	9	0.968	2	0.964
Sweden	5	0.976	3	0.957
Switzerland	4	0.977	4	0.957
Norway	3	0.978	5	0.956
Canada	1	0.982	6	0.947
Belgium	13	0.950	7	0.944
USA	6	0.976	8	0.943
United Kingdom	10	0.962	9	0.943
France	8	0.969	10	0.936
Australia	7	0.971	11	0.933
Finland	12	0.953	12	0.931
Denmark	11	0.953	13	0.923
Israel	15	0.939	14	0.913
New Zealand	14	0.947	15	0.909
Ireland	17	0.921	16	0.904
Spain	18	0.916	17	0.894
Italy	16	0.922	18	0.890
South Korea	21	0.871	19	0.884
Hungary	20	0.893	20	0.878
Hong Kong	19	0.913	21	0.871
Singapore	25	0.848	22	0.835
Yugoslavia	23	0.857	23	0.833
Costa Rica	26	0.842	24	0.820
Chile	22	0.863	25	0.817
Portugal	24	0.850	26	0.799
Argentina	27	0.833	27	0.792
Venezuela	28	0.824	28	0.771
Mauritius	30	0.793	29	0.744
Mexico	29	0.804	30	0.736
Malaysia	31	0.789	31	0.731
Colombia	32	0.758	32	0.722
Panama	34	0.731	33	0.648

Continued on next page

Country	HDI rank	HDI value	Income-distribution-adjusted HDI rank	value
Thailand	36	0.685	34	0.644
Brazil	33	0.739	35	0.635
Jamaica	35	0.722	36	0.631
Sri Lanka	39	0.651	37	0.623
Syria	38	0.665	38	0.617
Turkey	37	0.671	39	0.608
Philippines	40	0.600	40	0.572
Tunisia	41	0.582	41	0.566
Iran	42	0.547	42	0.510
Indonesia	44	0.491	43	0.495
El Salvador	43	0.498	44	0.483
Honduras	45	0.473	45	0.420
Egypt	46	0.385	46	0.373
Kenya	47	0.366	47	0.341
Pakistan	49	0.305	48	0.297
Zambia	48	0.315	49	0.292
India	50	0.297	50	0.278
Côte d'Ivoire	51	0.289	51	0.249
Bangladesh	52	0.185	52	0.168
Nepal	53	0.168	53	0.136

Source: UNDP, *Human Development Report 1992* (New York: Oxford University Press, 1992), Table 1.4, p. 22 and Table 1, pp 127–9.

GENDER-SENSITIVE HDIs

It is also possible to take gender discrimination into account when computing a country's HDI. Given the widespread discrimination against women, particularly in developing countries, a gender-sensitive HDI is potentially a useful tool of analysis for policymakers. In practice gender-sensitive HDIs have been computed by calculating an HDI in the usual way for the female population and a separate HDI for the male population. The ratio of the female to the male HDI is then multiplied by the country's overall HDI to produce a gender-sensitive Human Development Index (HDI_{gs}). Thus

$$HDI_{gs} = HDI_c \times \frac{HDI_{cf}}{HDI_{cm}} \text{ , where}$$

HDI_{cf} = the female HDI for country c, and
HDI_{cm} = the male HDI for country c.

In Table A1.2 we present gender-sensitive HDIs for the 33 countries for which sufficient data are available. We also present the ratio of the female HDI to the male HDI expressed as a percentage.

Table A1.2   The gender-sensitive HDI

Country	HDI_{gs}	HDI_{cf}/HDI_{cm}
Sweden	0.938	96.16
Norway	0.914	93.48
Finland	0.900	94.47
France	0.899	92.72
Denmark	0.879	92.20
Australia	0.879	90.48
New Zealand	0.851	89.95
Canada	0.842	85.73
USA	0.842	86.26
Netherlands	0.835	86.26
Belgium	0.822	86.57
Austria	0.822	86.47
United Kingdom	0.819	85.09
Czechoslovakia	0.810	90.25
Germany	0.796	83.32
Switzerland	0.790	80.92
Italy	0.772	83.83
Japan	0.761	77.56
Portugal	0.708	83.36
Luxembourg	0.695	74.88
Ireland	0.689	74.89
Greece	0.686	76.10
Cyprus	0.659	72.32
Hong Kong	0.649	71.10
Singapore	0.601	70.87
Costa Rica	0.595	70.61
South Korea	0.571	65.53
Paraguay	0.566	88.82
Sri Lanka	0.516	79.59
Philippines	0.472	78.67
Swaziland	0.315	68.74
Myanmar	0.285	74.07
Kenya	0.215	58.60

Source: UNDP, *Human Development Report 1992* (New York: Oxford University Press, 1992), Table 1.3, p. 21.

OTHER HDIs

As should by now be apparent, the HDI is a flexible tool of analysis which can be useful in monitoring the progress of human development. It can readily be disaggregated, assuming the data are available in the required form. In large countries with considerable geographical diversity, it might be useful to produce regional HDIs, using the same method applied to country HDIs. In pluralistic societies with ethnic diversity, it might be useful to produce an HDI for each ethnic group, using the same method used to produce female and male HDIs. In other words, the HDI can be disaggregated in a number of ways and each country can adapt it to suit its own policy purposes.

CHANGES IN THE HDI OVER TIME

The HDI ranks countries relative to each other for a particular year. The technical reason for this is that the maximum value for a country's I_l, I_k and I_y is determined by the maximum and minimum longevity, knowledge and income in the sample of countries being considered. This formulation contains an implicit assumption that HDI is a relative concept, not an absolute one. Hence it is possible for a country's longevity, knowledge and income to rise while its HDI falls. This would occur, for example, whenever the longevity, knowledge and income of other countries rose even faster than in the country concerned. Relative deterioration in the components of human development will result in a fall of a country's HDI even when there has been an absolute improvement.

Thus the HDI cannot be used to measure progress in human development over time. It is, however, easy to modify the HDI so that it can be used to record changes over time rather than a country's relative position at a given moment in time. All that need be done is to define L_{max} and L_{min}, R_{max} and R_{min}, S_{max} and S_{min}, Y_{max} and Y_{min} in (arbitrary) absolute terms. For example, L_{max} could be defined as a life expectancy of 90 years and L_{min} set at 30 years, and so on for the other variables. A country's HDI would then measure progress over time relative to the fixed but arbitrary maxima and minima. This procedure would make it possible in principle for all countries to record a rise in their HDI.

Those wishing to learn more about the construction of the HDI, criticisms that have been made of it and possible alternative formulations, should consult the *Human Development Report 1993*, Technical Notes 1 and 2.

Notes

Introduction

1. See, for example, UNDP, *Human Development Report 1990* (New York: Oxford University Press, 1990), Chapter 1. Also see the Appendix.

1   The Essential Features of a Human Development Strategy

1. See Amartya Sen, 'Development as Capability Expansion', in Keith Griffin and John Knight (eds), *Human Development and the International Development Strategy for the 1990s* (London: Macmillan, 1990).
2. For a demonstration of how this approach can be used to analyse human development in a specific country, see UNDP, *Balanced Development: An Approach to Social Action in Pakistan* (Islamabad, Pakistan, 1992).
3. The alternative to a benefit–cost approach is to specify specific targets (universal literacy, 75 per cent enrolment ratio in secondary education, reduction of the infant mortality rate by a quarter, etc.) and then to minimise the cost of attaining the targets. The advantages of specifying the targets in advance are, first, that the goals of the development strategy are clearly articulated and can be used to mobilise public support and, second, that the performance of the public administration can easily be monitored by comparing actual attainments with the specific targets. The disadvantages of target-setting are that the targets often are arbitrary, the costs of attaining one objective are not compared with the costs of attaining other objectives, and consequently the pattern of development expenditure may be inefficient and the overall rate of progress less than it otherwise would have been. See Chapter 4.
4. Methods for estimating environmental costs of economic activities are surveyed in Maureen L. Cropper and Wallace E. Oates, 'Environmental Economics: A Survey', *Journal of Economic Literature*, Vol. XXX, No. 2, June 1992.
5. See Keith Griffin, *Alternative Strategies for Economic Development* (London: Macmillan, 1989).
6. Paul Isenman, 'Basic Needs: The Case of Sri Lanka', *World Development*, Vol. 8, No. 3, March 1980.

2   The Structure of Incentives

1. Vali Jamal and John Weeks, 'The Vanishing Rural–Urban Gap in Sub-Saharan Africa', *International Labour Review*, Vol. 127, No. 3, 1988.
2. M. Aoki, 'Toward an Economic Model of the Japanese Firm', *Journal of Economic Literature*, Vol. 28, No. 1, 1990.
3. For a survey of the literature on interlinked markets see Pranab Bardhan,

'Interlocking Factor Markets and Agrarian Development: A Review of Issues', *Oxford Economic Papers*, March 1980.

4. See Michael D. Levin, 'Accountability and Legitimacy in Traditional Co-operation in Nigeria', in D. W. Attwood and B. S. Baviskar (eds), *Who Shares? Co-operatives and Rural Development* (Delhi: Oxford University Press, 1988).

5. See Mahabub Hossain, *Credit for the Rural Poor: The Grameen Bank in Bangladesh*, Bangladesh Institute of Development Studies Research Monograph No. 4, Dhaka, 1984. Also see Rushidon Islam Rahman, 'Poor Women's Access to Economic Gain from Grameen Bank Loans', Australian National University Research School of Pacific Studies, National Centre for Development Studies, Working Paper No. 91/2, 1991.

6. Douglas Southgate and Morris Whitaker, 'Promoting Resource Degradation in Latin America: Tropical Deforestation, Soil Erosion, and Coastal Ecosystem Disturbance in Ecuador', *Economic Development and Cultural Change*, July 1992.

7. Hernando de Soto, *The Other Path* (New York: Harper and Row, 1989).

8. Ibid. Legal restraints on the development of the informal sector were first called to the attention of a wide audience in ILO, *Employment, Incomes and Equality: A Strategy for Increasing Productive Employment in Kenya*, 1972.

9. See, for example, R. Repetto and M. Gillis (eds), *Public Policies and the Misuse of Forest Resources* (Cambridge: Cambridge University Press, 1988).

10. D. Mahar, *Government Policies and Deforestation in Brazil's Amazon Region* (Washington, DC: World Bank, 1989).

11. See Keith Griffin and Azizur Rahman Khan, *Globalization and the Developing World: an Essay on the International Dimensions of Development in the Post-Cold War Era* (Geneva: UNRISD, 1992), p. 20.

12. Ibid., p. 21.

13. Keith Griffin, *Alternative Strategies for Economic Development* (London: Macmillan, 1989), Chapter 6.

14. UNDP, *Balanced Development: An Approach to Social Action in Pakistan* (Islamabad, Pakistan, 1992).

15. Nathan Rosenberg, *Perspectives on Technology* (London: Cambridge University Press, 1987), pp. 192–3.

16. Aaron Segal, 'From Technology Transfer to Science and Technology Institutionalization', in John R. McIntyre and Daniel S. Papp (eds), *The Political Economy of International Technology Transfer* (Westport, Connecticut: Quorum Books, 1986).

17. Kenneth J. Arrow, 'The Economic Implications of Learning by Doing', *Review of Economic Studies*, No. 29, 1962, pp. 155–73.

18. Nathan Rosenberg, *Inside the Black Box: Technology and Economics* (Cambridge, Mass.: Cambridge University Press, 1982).

19. This whole section draws on the discussion in Edward J. Malecki, *Technology and Economic Development: The Dynamics of Local, Regional and National Change* (New York: Longman, 1991), Chapter 4.

20. Aaron Segal, 'Africa: Frustration and Failure', in Aaron Segal (ed.), *Learning By Doing: Science and Technology in the Developing World* (Boulder, Colorado: Westview Press, 1987).

21. There is evidence from developing as well as developed countries that public

and private investment are complementary rather than substitutes for one another. See, for example, Eliana Cardoso, 'Private Investment in Latin America', *Economic Development and Cultural Change*, Vol. 41, No. 4, July 1993 and C. Lynde and J. Richmond, 'Public Capital and Long-run Costs in U.K. Manufacturing', *Economic Journal*, Vol. 103, No. 419, July 1993.

3 Reallocation of Public Sector Resources

1. Giovanni Andrea Cornia and Frances Stewart, 'Two Errors of Targeting', UNICEF, International Child Development Centre, Florence, Italy, Innocenti Occasional Papers, EPS 36, March 1993.
2. The expression comes from the title of a book by Giovanni Andrea Cornia, Richard Jolly and Frances Stewart (eds), *Adjustment with a Human Face* (Oxford: Clarendon Press, 1987).
3. See UNDP, *Balanced Development: An Approach to Social Action in Pakistan*, loc. cit. and UNDP, *Human Development in Bangladesh* (Dhaka, Bangladesh, 1992).
4. The inverted pyramid applies not only to public expenditure on formal education but also to health, pensions, public food distribution, transportation (compare air travel with farm-to-market roads), irrigation (compare expenditures on large-scale water management projects with small-scale irrigation facilities), industrial support, etc. In each case expenditure per beneficiary increases as one climbs the pyramid while net social returns tend to fall. Thus the point made in the text about the composition of educational expenditure has wide applicability to other sectors.
5. For example, in Indonesia in 1978 it is estimated that 83 per cent of state subsidies to higher education accrued to the upper-income group, 10 per cent to the middle-income group and only 7 per cent to the lower-income group. Indonesia is perhaps an extreme case, but a similar pattern is evident in Chile, Colombia and Malaysia. See George Psacharopoulos, 'Education and Development: A Review', *World Bank Research Observer*, Vol. 3, No. 1, January 1988, Table 5, p. 104.
6. Excluding China and India, which have good records, the primary school enrolment rate in the 'other low-income economies' was 77 per cent in 1989. In the 'middle-income economies' the enrolment rate was 101 per cent. See World Bank, *World Development Report 1992* (New York: Oxford University Press, 1992).
7. In Africa, for example, the rates of return on investments in education are estimated to be 26 per cent for primary education, 17 per cent for secondary education, and 13 per cent for higher education. These rates of return include public subsidies in total costs but make no attempt to include positive externalities in the benefits. Thus they understate the true social rates of return. See George Psacharopoulos, op. cit., Table 1, p. 101. On the other hand, it has been argued that in some cases the procedures used for calculating rates of return to expenditure on education result in overestimates of the true rates of return. See, for example, Jere R. Behrman and Anil B. Deolalikar, 'Unobserved Household and Community Heterogeneity and the Labor Market Impact of Schooling: A

134 *Notes*

Case Study for Indonesia', *Economic Development and Cultural Change*, Vol. 41, No. 3, April 1993.

8. For a study of urban areas in East Africa, see John Knight and Richard Sabot, 'Educational Policy and Labour Productivity: An Output Accounting Exercise', *Economic Journal*, Vol. 97, No. 385, March 1987; and, for a study of rural areas in Latin America, see Daniel Cotlear, 'The Effects of Education on Farm Productivity', in Keith Griffin and John Knight (eds), op. cit. Also see Marlaine E. Lockheed, Dean T. Jamison and Lawrence J. Lau, 'Farmer Education and Farm Efficiency: A Survey', *Economic Development and Cultural Change*, October 1980.

9. UNDP, *Human Development Report 1992* (New York: Oxford University Press, 1992).

10. UNDP, *Balanced Development: An Approach to Social Action in Pakistan*, loc. cit.

11. See UNDP, *Human Development in Bangladesh*, loc. cit. and UNDP, *Making People Matter: Introductory Comment on a Human Development Strategy for Ghana*, Accra, Ghana, draft June 1992.

12. Mark Hopkins was a distinguished teacher at Williams College, Massachusetts in the nineteenth century.

13. All the data in this paragraph were obtained from John Oxenham with Jocelyn DeJong and Steven Treagust, 'Improving the Quality of Education in Developing Countries', in Keith Griffin and John Knight (eds), op. cit.

14. This is now widely recognised. See, for instance, the World Bank, *World Development Report 1993* (New York: Oxford University Press, 1993), which is devoted to 'Investing in Health'.

15. UNDP, *Human Development in Bangladesh*, loc. cit.

16. See Amartya Sen, *Poverty and Famines: An Essay on Entitlement and Deprivation* (Oxford: Oxford University Press, 1981); and Jean Drèze and Amartya Sen, *Hunger and Public Action* (Oxford: Oxford University Press, 1989).

17. Thienchay Kiranandana and Kraisid Tontisirin, *Eradicating Child Malnutrition: Thailand's Health, Nutrition and Poverty Alleviation Policy in the 1980s*, UNICEF, International Child Development Centre, Innocenti Occasional Papers, Economic Policy Series, No. 23, January 1992.

18. For a discussion of hospital user fees in practice in the Dominican Republic, Honduras and Jamaica see Maureen A. Lewis, 'User Fees in Public Hospitals: Comparison of Three Case Studies', *Economic Development and Cultural Change*, Vol. 41, No. 3, April 1993.

19. Keith Griffin, op. cit., pp. 50–59.

20. James Boyce, 'The Revolving Door? External Debt and Capital Flight: A Philippine Case Study', *World Development*, Vol. 20, No. 3, March 1992.

21. Hans Singer, 'Beyond the Debt Crisis', *Development* (the journal of the Society for International Development), No. 1, 1992.

22. Daniel P. Hewett, 'Military Expenditures in the Developing World', *Finance and Development*, Vol. 28, No. 3, September 1991.

23. Saadet Deger and Somnath Sen, *Military Expenditure: The Political Economy of International Security*, Stockholm International Peace Research Institute (New York: Oxford University Press, 1990).

24. Robert S. McNamara, 'Reducing Military Expenditures in the Third World', *Finance and Development*, Vol. 28, No. 3, September 1991.
25. Saadat Deger and Somneth Sen, op. cit.
26. Daniel P. Hewett, op. cit.
27. Robert S. McNamara, op. cit.
28. Fundación para la Educación Superior y el Desarrollo, *Un Plan de Desarrollo Humano de Largo Plazo para Colombia* (Bogotá, Colombia, 1992).
29. In some cases where outright private ownership is not desirable, e.g. because of absence of competition, it might be possible to combine private ownership with tight government regulation of the enterprise. Whether this formula is preferable to public ownership depends in part on the cost, often very high, of creating and sustaining an efficient regulatory framework.
30. See Janos Kornai, *Economics of Shortage*, 2 vols (New York: North-Holland, 1980).
31. See, for example, Alan Whitworth, 'Public Enterprise Reform in Papua New Guinea', *World Development*, Vol. 20, No. 1, January 1992. In the case of utility companies, user charges can be used to eliminate excess demand and if they are differentiated by income group, they can be used to achieve equitable access. See, for example, Samuel Paul, 'Privatization and the Public Sector', *Finance and Development*, Vol. 22, No. 4, December 1985.
32. In Karachi, Pakistan, for example, the benefits of Provincial and Municipal expenditures on transportation, education, health, law and order, water supply and roads are nearly four times larger for the highest income group than for the lowest. See Aisha Ghaus, 'The Incidence of Public Expenditure in Karachi', *Pakistan Journal of Applied Economics*, Vol. VIII, No. 1, Summer 1989, Table 2, p. 98.
33. Marvin Taylor-Dormond, 'The State and Poverty in Costa Rica', *Cepal Review*, No. 43, 1991.
34. Fundación para la Educación Superior y el Desarrollo, op. cit., Bogotá, March 1992.
35. See P. N. Dhar, 'Economic Reforms: Why We Need Them', Observer Research Foundation, New Delhi, India, Occasional Paper, March 1992.
36. Raymond Z. H. Renfro, 'Fertilizer Price and Subsidy Policies in Bangladesh', *World Development*, Vol. 20, No. 3, March 1992.
37. K. Subbarao, 'State Policies and Regional Disparity in Indian Agriculture', *Development and Change*, Vol. 16, No. 4, October 1985.
38. Douglas H. Graham, Howard Gauthier and Jose Roberto Mendonca, 'Thirty Years of Agricultural Growth in Brazil: Crop Performance, Regional Profile and Recent Policy Review', *Economic Development and Cultural Change*, Vol. 36, No. 1, October 1987.
39. See UNDP, *Human Development Report 1991* (New York: Oxford University Press, 1991), Chapter 3.

5 Structural Reforms

1. Amartya Sen, *Employment, Technology and Development* (London: Oxford University Press, 1975).

2. The experience of the International Labour Organisation in supporting such projects, particularly in Africa, is evaluated in Jacques Gaude and Steve Miller, 'Rural Development and Local Resource Intensity: A Case-Study Approach', in Keith Griffin and John Knight (eds), op. cit.

3. See, for example, Thomas G. Rawski, *Economic Growth and Employment in China* (New York: Oxford University Press, 1979).

4. See, for example, Sarthi Acharya, *The Maharashtra Employment Guarantee Scheme: A Study of Labour Market Intervention*, New Delhi: ILO, ARTEP, Working Paper, May 1990.

5. UNDP, *Human Development in Bangladesh*, loc. cit., p. 25.

6. Issues of participation and empowerment within the context of a human development strategy are ably discussed in Dharam Ghai, 'Participatory Development: Some Perspectives from Grass-Roots Experiences', in Keith Griffin and John Knight (eds), op. cit.

7. UNDP, *Human Development in Bangladesh*, loc. cit., p. 8.

8. Inderjit Singh, *The Great Ascent: The Rural Poor in South Asia* (Baltimore: Johns Hopkins University Press, 1990), p. 55.

9. Ibid., p. 61.

10. See, for example, Keith Griffin, *The Political Economy of Agrarian Change* (London: Macmillan, 1974).

11. John C. H. Fei, Gustav Ranis and Shirley W. Y. Kuo, *Growth and Equity: The Taiwan Case* (New York: Oxford University Press, 1979).

12. Sung Yeung Kwack, 'The Economic Development of the Republic of Korea, 1965–1981', in Lawrence J. Lau (ed), *Models of Development: A Comparative Study of Economic Growth in South Korea and Taiwan* (San Francisco: Institute for Contemporary Studies, 1986).

13. Byung-Nak Song, *The Rise of the Korean Economy* (New York: Oxford University Press, 1990).

14. Terry McKinley, 'The Distribution of Wealth in Rural China', in Keith Griffin and Zhao Renwei (eds), *The Distribution of Income in China* (London: Macmillan, 1993).

15. See, for example, Jere R. Behrman and Anil B. Deolalikar, 'Will Developing Country Nutrition Improve with Income? A Case Study for Rural South India', *Journal of Political Economy*, Vol. 95, No. 3, 1987.

16. See, for example, Anil B. Deolalikar, 'Nutrition and Labor Productivity in Agriculture: Estimates for Rural South India', *Review of Economics and Statistics*, Vol. LXX, No. 3, August 1988.

17. The discussion below was influenced by Partha Dasgupta, 'The Economics of Destitution', Development Economics Research Programme, London School of Economics, STICERD Discussion Paper No. 43, January 1993.

18. See Per Pinstrup-Andersen, 'Targeted Nutrition Interventions', *Food and Nutrition Bulletin*, Vol. 13, No. 3, September 1991.

19. Amartya Sen, 'Public Action to Remedy Hunger', the fourth annual Arturo Tanco Memorial Lecture, London: The Global Hunger Project, 1990, p. 21.

20. Ibid.

21. The advantages and disadvantages of various forms of food rationing and price controls are discussed in Keith Griffin and Jeffrey James, *The Transition to Egalitarian Development* (London: Macmillan, 1981), Chapter 4.

22. Our discussion of human development and economic security is strongly influenced by Ehtisham Ahmad, Jean Drèze and Amartya Sen (eds), *Social Security in Developing Countries* (Oxford: Clarendon Press, 1991).
23. See Nicholas Barr, 'Economic Theory and the Welfare State: A Survey and Interpretation', *Journal of Economic Literature*, Vol. XXX, No. 2, June 1992.
24. Ibid., Table 1, p. 759. The figures refer to 1980.
25. Ibid., Table 5, p. 775. The data refer to the mid-1980s.
26. Ibid., Table 6, p. 776. The data refer to the early 1980s.
27. Ehtisham Ahmad, Jean Drèze and Amartya Sen (eds), op. cit.
28. S. Guhan, 'Social Security for the Unorganised Poor: A Feasible Blueprint for India', paper presented to a Symposium on Economic Growth, Sustainable Human Development and Poverty Alleviation in India, Indira Gandhi Institute of Development Research, Bombay, 3–6 January 1992.
29. Ibid., pp. 23–32.

6 Human Development and Sustainable Development

1. See, for example, James K. Boyce, 'Towards a Political Economy of Sustainable Development', Department of Economics, University of Massachusetts, Amherst, Working Paper 1993–8.
2. See for example, R. Repetto, W. Magrath, M. Wells, C. Beer and F. Rossini, *Wasting Assets: Natural Resources in the National Income Accounts* (World Resources Institute, Washington, D.C., 1989).
3. This leaves unanswered the difficult question of how changes in the stock of natural capital are to be valued. Various techniques have been developed, e.g. estimates of how much people would be prepared to pay for an environmental service or how much they would be prepared to accept for the loss of an environmental service, none of which are fully satisfactory. The crucial point, however, is a conceptual one: changes in the stock of natural capital should be subject in principle to what we have called in the text the calculus of benefits and costs.
4. Olman Segura Bonilla and James K. Boyce, 'Investing in Natural and Human Capital in Developing Countries', paper presented at the Second Meeting of the International Society for Ecological Economics, Stockholm, August 1992, p. 6.
5. Ibid.
6. *BioScience*, Vol. 42, No. 4, April 1992, p. 325.
7. Jan Pronk and Mahbub ul Haq, *Sustainable Development: From Concept to Action* (New York: UNDP, March 1992), p. 9.

7 Finance and Administration

1. Malcolm Gillis, 'Comprehensive Tax Reform: The Indonesian Experience, 1981–1988', in Malcolm Gillis (ed.), *Tax Reform in Developing Countries* (Duke University Press, 1989).
2. Charles E. McLure, Jr., 'Income Tax Reform in Colombia and Venezuela: A Comparative History', *World Development*, Vol. 20, No. 3, March 1992.

3. Malcolm Gillis, 'Tax Reform: Lessons from Postwar Experience in Developing Nations', in Malcolm Gillis (ed.), op. cit.
4. James Alm, Roy Bahl and Matthew N. Murray, 'Tax Base Erosion in Developing Countries', *Economic Development and Cultural Change*, Vol. 39, No. 4, July 1991.
5. David Newberry, 'Agricultural Taxation: The Main Issues', in David Newberry and Nicholas Stern (eds), *The Theory of Taxation for Developing Countries* (New York: Oxford University Press, 1987).
6. Malcolm Gillis, 'Comprehensive Tax Reform: The Indonesia Experience, 1981–1988', loc. cit.
7. Richard M. Bird and Barbara Diane Miller, 'The Incidence of Indirect Taxes on Low-Income Households in Jamaica', *Economic Development and Cultural Change*, Vol. 37, No. 2, January 1989.
8. Richard M. Bird, *Tax Policy and Economic Development* (Baltimore: Johns Hopkins University Press, 1992).
9. UNDP, *Human Development Report 1992* (New York: Oxford University Press, 1992).
10. World Bank, *World Development Report 1992* (New York: Oxford University Press, 1992), Table 9, pp. 234–5.
11. This argument is developed in Keith Griffin and Azizur Rahman Khan, *Globalization and the Developing World* (Geneva: United Nations Research Institute for Social Development, 1992), Chapter 4.
12. Keith Griffin, 'Foreign Aid After the Cold War', *Development and Change*, Vol. 22, No. 4, October 1991.
13. See the valuable discussion in Joel Samoff, 'Decentralization: The Politics of Interventionism', *Development and Change*, Vol. 21, No. 3, July 1990.
14. Ibid.
15. Henry Bienen, Devesh Kapur, James Parks and Jeffrey Riedinger, 'Decentralization in Nepal', *World Development,* Vol. 18, No. 1, January 1990.
16. See Dharam Ghai, 'Participatory Development: Some Perspectives from Grass-Roots Experiences', loc. cit.
17. UNDP, *Human Development in Bangladesh*, loc. cit.
18. For an interesting study of government decentralisation, participation and local development, see Neil Webster, 'Panchayati Raj in West Bengal: Popular Participation for the People or the Party?', *Development and Change*, Vol. 23, No.4, October 1992.

Index

Index

i

DATE DUE